CHARCOAL

NEW WAYS TO COOK WITH FIRE

CHARCOAL

JOSIAH CITRIN

-&-

JOANN CIANCIULLI

AVERY

an imprint of Penguin Random House LLC
penguinrandomhouse.com

Most Avery books are available at special quantity discounts
for bulk purchase for sales promotions, premiums, fund-
raising, and educational needs. Special books or book
excerpts also can be created to fit specific needs. For details,
write SpecialMarkets@penguinrandomhouse.com.

Library of Congress Cataloging-in-Publication Data
Names: Citrin, Josiah, author. | Cianciulli, JoAnn, author.
Title: Charcoal : new ways to cook with fire /
Josiah Citrin and JoAnn Cianciulli.
Description: New York : Avery, an imprint of Penguin
Random House, [2019] | Includes index.
Identifiers: LCCN 2018058131| ISBN 9780525534792
(hardcover) | ISBN 9780525534808 (ebook)
Subjects: LCSH: Barbecuing. | Outdoor cooking. |
LCGFT: Cookbooks.
Classification: LCC TX840.B3 C57 2019 |
DDC 641.5/78—dc23
LC record available at https://lccn.loc.gov/2018058131
p   cm.

Printed in the United States of America
1 3 5 7 9 10 8 6 4 2

Book design by Ashley Tucker

To my children, Augie and Olivia,
my girlfriend, Samantha, and my
parents, Huli, Michel, and Raphael

CONTENTS

FOREWORD

The first meal I ever enjoyed in Los Angeles was at Mélisse, where I met Josiah. I think we are innately attracted to someone with a kindred background and that's why I was immediately fond of him. Josiah and I both trained in Europe, we both opened fine dining restaurants in L.A., and then went on to open restaurants that play with fire.

We all have this image of the fine dining chef. He looks like the guy in the Lindt chocolate ads with his funny hat. Josiah is brave enough to strip away the pretense and just cook in a way that is unexpected of him and how I know he enjoys cooking at home. The results are unbelievable.

It's an interesting thing. To me, there is something about lighting a fire and watching people gather around it that warms the soul. Whether it's to keep off the chill or to stand around with a beer and tend to food being cooked, trust me, when you light that fire, people gravitate to it. Top that by cooking some interesting things over it and feeding people—well, you've got an awesome experience. Josiah has taken that plus all of his knowledge and training and has created it for his guests at his fabulous restaurant Charcoal. He has no fear in saying, "Yeah, I'm going to bury a cabbage under a bunch of coal and it's going to taste delicious!"

He masters the flame. How Josiah's Liberty duck with crisp skin and succulence is enacted in a kitchen that simultaneously is cooking up some smoky chicken wings (and what chicken wings!) on a Big Green Egg is a thing of beauty. That duck is the dish I have literally woken up in the middle of the night thinking about. Then there is all the veg. I have never seen vegetarians so over the moon about dining in a meat-focused restaurant. It's all because Josiah reveres and respects the ingredients. Whether it's grilled orata with an herby yogurt, a porcini-dusted New York strip, or that insane cabbage dish I mentioned baked in embers with sumac and lemon zest, flavor is the bottom line to these dishes.

You're in for a treat with these recipes. They're not only achievable, they're downright delicious, inclusive of all the wonderful seasonal produce we lucky devils are privy to here. But I always suggest, use what's available at the farmers' market and you can't go wrong. Josiah guides you with alternatives and swaps for ingredients that may not be accessible to you. And here's a not-so-secret secret, I have a crazy sweet tooth (just ask my dentist). There really isn't a tastier dessert than fruit smoked over fire. Let that sink in when you're sipping on my favorite cocktail recipe, the Midnight Margarita. So gather your mates like a moth to a flame and get cooking.

What's that old adage? Where there's smoke, there's fire. Well, where there's Charcoal, there is Josiah. Proud of you, mate. Now, when are you having me over for dinner?

CURTIS STONE,
chef and owner of Maude and Gwen Butcher Shop & Restaurant

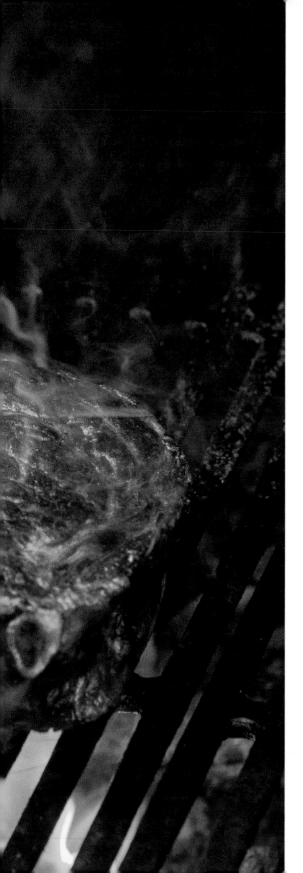

CHARCOAL AND FIRE

"Let Fire Fuel Your Passion" is our mantra at Charcoal with good reason. The restaurant is extremely personal to me, born from my desire to share the wood-fired foods I cook at home on Sundays in a fun, communal restaurant where all are welcome. The idea behind Charcoal was planted in my mind twenty years ago when, as a young chef training in France, I frequented a little restaurant in Basque country called La Tantina de Burgos. The menu was straightforward—grilled meats, fish, and vegetables accompanied by a selection of vinegars and table condiments served on the side—but there was just something magical about the fire-kissed foods, the smell of charcoal, and the boisterous atmosphere that stayed with me over the years.

After returning home to Los Angeles in the early '90s and working the charcoal grill station at Wolfgang Puck's iconic Chinois on Main, among other renowned places, I set out on my own with the goal of launching a fine dining restaurant, and opened Mélisse in 1999. Undeniably, Mélisse is fancy and French. Boasting an elegant tasting menu, white tablecloths, and world-class service, the restaurant exemplifies the core of my formal training and unwavering attention to detail and execution. I'm beyond proud of what we have achieved, and the pursuit of excellence is an integral part of who I am as a chef and restaurateur. I love sautéing in shiny copper pots, wearing a crisp-pressed chef's coat, celebrating milestone occasions with our guests, and delivering a memorable dining experience. Mélisse has gone on to earn multiple awards, including a coveted two-star Michelin rating, and I'm grateful it continues to be regarded as a dining destination after two decades (not an easy feat given the ever-evolving restaurant climate in Los Angeles).

But Mélisse is not the kind of place where friends can casually pop in for a quick drink and a bite to eat, and the multicourse tasting menu is contrary to what I actually cook at home. At a certain point, I reached a stage in my career when I yearned for another creative outlet and to cook food that was more soulful and personal. Don't get me wrong, fine dining has its place and is truly rewarding on many levels, but I felt the urge to balance both sides of who I am as a professional chef, and to satisfy the guy who loves cooking with his Big Green Egg grill and smoker for family and friends at his house by the beach.

The Charcoal concept clicked when I dined at Nancy Silverton's outstanding Italian steak house, Chi Spacca, on Melrose Avenue. Memories of that little Basque restaurant flooded back, and I was also reminded of the casual barbecue gatherings I love to have, where we pass around platters of charred meats, vegetables, and seafood at the table family-style and there's lots of laughter in the air. I realized that there was a beautiful opportunity to create a restaurant with wood and fire at its heart, where food is best shared, and I became driven to capture that experience and spirit. It all felt instinctive to me and, before long, the feeling became a reality.

Charcoal opened a stone's throw from Venice Beach in 2015, and the journey has been incredibly liberating for me both professionally and personally. Part of being a chef is caring for people, and from the beginning I wanted Charcoal to feel like it had always been part of the Venice neighborhood, a friendly place where the food and people come together with warmth and vibrancy. Cooking with fire doesn't just add flavor to food, it creates community and connection. It naturally brings people together.

Charcoal is a grill restaurant—not a steak house—and it's a place where carnivores can share a meal with their vegetarian friends. I firmly believe that when treated with respect, vegetables can satisfy anyone who simply enjoys good food. In fact, one of our most popular and critically acclaimed dishes on the menu is our Cabbage Baked in Embers with Yogurt, Sumac, and Lemon Zest (page 133). Having grown up in California, where there is an abundance of fresh produce, heavily influences the way I cook and it's the reason much of our menu gives vegetable-driven dishes equal billing with our meat offerings. For me, it's not just grilling a big slab of meat—I also use fire to showcase the nuances of vegetables—their varied color, texture, and flavor. Vegetables are the catalyst for true innovation. They require a different kind of finesse, and the cooking process is more of an adventure. I love to create simple vegetable dishes with complex, contrasting flavors like Coal-Roasted Carrots with Ricotta, Herbs, and Black Pepper Honey (page 138), which features charred carrots glazed with sweet and spicy honey, topped with cool

creamy cheese and fresh herbs. The layers of flavor are as delicious as they are unexpected. Or Smoked Strawberries with Strawberry Water and Basil (page 217), which uses wood and smoke for an unusual cooking preparation that imparts robust flavor. My vegetable dishes can even shine on their own as the star of the meal (see Grilled Chopped Vegetable Salad with Havarti, Bacon, Kalamata Olives, and Jo-Jo's Vinaigrette on page 61).

As a chef living and cooking in Los Angeles, it's easy to take for granted the bounty of fresh produce I have access to. You will find me at the Santa Monica Farmers Market every Wednesday morning—developing and cultivating relationships with local farmers and purveyors is a special privilege of being a chef in L.A. I cannot think of too many other places that can match the accessibility to such plentiful ingredients as we have in California. I'm a firm believer in seasonality and eating what's good *when* it's good. No matter where you live, always choose the best-quality ingredients and enjoy them during their growing season. For instance, Corn Elote with Lime, Chili, Cilantro, and Cotija Cheese (page 148) is best when corn is at its peak in the summer, and Grilled Asparagus with Chopped Egg Vinaigrette (page 73) is finest in springtime, when asparagus is thriving. Farmer's markets are your friends. Eat local and in season when you can.

Gathering around a fire to eat and share stories is as much a ritual today as it was when the earliest humans did it thousands of years ago. It is a craving deep in our DNA. People around the globe have their own unique way of cooking over live fire. In the American South, barbecue reigns supreme. Argentina is known for *asado*; Japanese cooks use *teppanyaki* and *yakatori* grills; Korea is famous for *galbi*; and in the Middle East and Thailand you'll find meat cooked on sticks known as *shish kebab* and *satay*, respectively. There are more examples than I can list here, but the basic fundamentals are the same: fire, smoke, food, people gathering together, and a celebration of the rich flavor that no other cooking method can achieve.

Mastering the heat of the grill improves with practice. The best way to cook over live fire is to do so often right in your own backyard. It's a total sensory experience—you must engage your taste, touch, hearing, sight, and smell to elevate your grilling game. And doing so will make you a smarter cook overall. Think of your coal bed as a series of stove burners and use the same sensory cues you use when cooking food in a pan—the smell and look of food as it browns, how an ingredient shrinks, the way it feels to the touch, and how loudly it sizzles—to guide you. The process cannot be rushed—the temperature of fire is constantly changing, and there are so many varying factors, like weather, wind, and type of charcoal, that come into play. Every charcoal fire is one-of-a-kind and part of the attraction lies in the challenge of responding to the way it is burning. It is rewarding to be in the moment and engage with the fire with no distractions.

This cookbook is about craveability, dishes I hope you'll make again and again and want to generously share with friends and family. I've structured the chapters in a way that makes sense to me—by cooking method, including

Santa Monica Farmers Market with Joe Johnson (left) and Ken Takayama (center)

straightforward grilling over direct heat, cooking right on the coals, using red-hot coals to lightly char, and wood smoking. My goal is to show you how to utilize the coals in different ways to maximize the versatility of your grill and introduce you to new techniques and flavors. In the restaurant (and this book) the dishes are meant to be mixed and matched and enjoyed family-style. I encourage you to pick and choose what dishes sound complementary to one another and to cook in season. However, for ease, I also offer serving suggestions throughout to help guide you. The recipes are doable for every skill level and are full of essential accents that help bring balance to grill-centric meals. For example, pungent chimichurri, acidic vinaigrettes, and flavorful spice rubs and sauces provide the building blocks of flavor to support, not mask, the seductive smoky flavor you inherently get from cooking with fire.

To be sure, *Charcoal* is not a "quick and easy" cookbook, but the recipes are not overwhelming either. While all of the recipes have been written and tested with the home cook in mind, they are not watered-down versions of those we make in the restaurant. As with most meals, planning ahead will save you time, whether it's marinating meat the night before, roasting vegetables a couple of hours in advance, or keeping a well-stocked pantry so you can think on your feet any day of the week. With few exceptions, most of the ingredients called for in the recipes are widely available at any major grocery store. You don't need to scour the Internet for crazy, hard-to-get ingredients or kitchen equipment, and for anything slightly out of the ordinary, such as Piment d'Espelette (page 34) and fermented black beans (page 46), I've included ingredient notes on where to purchase them and suggested substitutes. As with most ingredients, though, the better quality you start with—whether it's olive oil or produce—the better your result on the plate.

Cooking outside over live fire is as much about connecting with people as it is about food. A meal prepared outdoors invites everyone to relax and enjoy heaping family-style platters, good drinks (and sometimes my secret stash of bourbon), and easy conversation. So let's fire up the coals!

BEFORE YOU BEGIN

This section walks you through what you need to make the recipes in this book. The first rule is: Get organized! Have everything you need for grilling—the food, salt, peppermill, cutting board, knife, side platters or baking pans for resting, and any other necessary equipment—on hand and ready at grill side before you light the first coal. You don't want to leave your grill unattended while you run to and from the kitchen, searching for and grabbing things you need. Organization will free you up to enjoy your outdoor cooking experience and your guests. But first let's talk about the heart of this type of cooking: the grill itself.

GRILLS

I like to think of my grill as the centerpiece of my outdoor kitchen rather than just another cooking tool. All of the recipes were developed and tested on the two most common charcoal grill types: the kettle grill and the Kamado. While gas grills are convenient, they don't allow for coal roasting, and you simply cannot achieve the same fiery flavor with a propane tank.

Kettle Grill

The most popular kettle grill on the market is commonly called by the brand name Weber. While the iconic backyard staple is terrific for cooking hamburgers and hot dogs on the Fourth of July, this lightweight, affordable charcoal grill can also be converted into a smoker with skillful vent control and the addition of wood chunks. The round design focuses heat and the multiple vents allow you to custom control the airflow. For under $200, you can purchase the standard 22-inch size. (I don't recommend the 18-inch version, as I find the grilling surface too small.) Once the grill is cool, be sure to clean excess debris and ash out of the kettle bowl to keep the bottom vents clear from clogging.

Kamado Grill

Known for its distinctive green color and oval shape, the Big Green Egg gave this heavy-duty ceramic grill a significant cult following. *Kamado* is the Japanese word for "stove" or "cooking range" and the vessel is a distant cousin to the Indian tandoor. The word has become a generic term for this style of ceramic cooker. We have several Big Green Eggs at Charcoal and I personally have one in my own backyard, and it frankly does a hell of a job cooking. What makes this grill so popular is that the insulated heat of the ceramic shell can produce high temperatures *and* it can also hold low temperatures, making it a legit smoker. The deep cylindrical shape is designed to hold more coal, which makes it perfect for long smokes or cooks, so you don't have to keep adding more coals to sustain the fire, and the super-thick walls maintain the temperature and heat accuracy for hours. The temperature is controlled by two adjustable vents: an opening on the bottom that provides air to the charcoal and a controllable vent in the top of the dome lid that allows air and smoke to exit. Now for the bad news: Kamado grills don't come cheap and are heavy, but if you love cooking with charcoal, they really are my favorite.

No matter which type of charcoal grill you own or purchase, make sure the vents are open when you set up the grill and light your charcoal. When you are done cooking, simply close the lid and vents and let the lack of oxygen kill the fire. This will stop the remaining coals from burning any further and the coals left behind can be relit for the next cookout. After each use, brush the cooking grate off with a dry, sturdy grill brush while hot to keep it clean and ready for the next go-around.

CHARCOAL

Natural hardwood lump charcoal is made entirely of wood and the only thing I use when cooking with fire. All charcoal is made of the same thing: wood burned with little oxygen so that all that's left is essentially carbon. It contains no additives like regular briquettes or, worse, instant-light ones saturated with lighter fluid. I use a mix of oak and hickory woods. Whatever brand you choose, make sure the bag says 100 percent natural with no additives whatsoever.

OTHER TOOLS AND EQUIPMENT

Whether I'm cooking in a kitchen or outdoors, I don't use a lot of extraneous equipment and gadgets. I'm not a fan of those packaged barbecue tool sets and prefer to buy utensils and tools individually. I find it's best to spend money on quality ingredients rather than on a bunch of accessories. So when it comes to essential barbecue tools, my list is pretty straightforward.

Tongs—I like to have a couple of sizes of heavy-duty stainless-steel kitchen tongs without silicone heads. I use long 12-inch tongs for managing food and moving around the coals and a medium-length 9-inch pair to lift the grill grate and for when I need a bit more stability.

Spatula—A large metal turning spatula is good to have on hand for turning food. Again, always use stainless steel with long handles and comfortable heatproof grips to ensure the spatula won't melt or warp from the heat and to keep your arms at a safe distance from the fire.

Garden Tools—A short metal rake, hoe, and shovel are also useful to shift around the coals at times. To load and unload the charcoal from the grill, I use a small shovel and rake; these garden tools are especially useful when building a cooking bed for any dish made in the coals (see "In the Coals," page 128). When purchasing, make sure the handles are made of wood instead of plastic to prevent them from melting.

Grill Brush—It is important to start with a clean grill to get better grill marks and to keep food from sticking, so make cleaning a part of your routine every single time you use your grill. When buying a grill brush, invest in a sturdy one with a long handle and heavy bristles that won't easily fall out. Get into the habit of scrubbing your grill right after you use it while the grate is hot to remove any food particles or burnt-on bits. It only takes a minute or two and you can do it while your food is resting. If not possible, be sure to clean the grill before you use it again while the grate is hot and prepped for the next cookout. In a pinch, you can use a wadded-up ball of aluminum foil to clean your grill, but I do not recommend this makeshift alternative as a regular practice. Note: Grill brushes don't last forever—when the bristles begin to look singed and worn down, it's time to buy a new one.

Side Towels—You can never have enough dry kitchen towels when cooking on your grill. I use them to wipe my hands and utensils and for handling hot food. You don't need the finest cotton for this; a raggedy towel that you don't mind getting dirty serves its purpose here.

Thermometers—I suggest having two types of thermometers: a digital instant-read thermometer to check the internal temperature of meat, and a laser infrared thermometer for checking the temperature of the grill itself.

Digital Instant-Read Thermometer—The only foolproof way to deliver perfectly cooked meat to the table is by using an instant-read thermometer. To use an instant-read thermometer, you simply stick the probe into the thickest part of the meat, and wait until you have the internal temperature reading, which takes only about 3 seconds. Once you have the temperature, remove the probe and either keep cooking or take your meat off the heat if it's done. Digital thermometers are not only for cooking on a grill but also a vital tool in the kitchen. A good one will run you about $30 and will last for many years (battery life is anywhere from 3,000 to 5,000 hours). When using a digital instant-read thermometer, you'll need to calibrate it soon after you buy it to be sure the reading is accurate. To do so, fill a tall glass with ice cubes, add cold water, and let it sit a couple of minutes. Insert the probe and make sure the tip is not touching the ice. The temperature should read 32°F.

Laser Infrared Thermometer—Shaped like a gun with a built-in laser, infrared thermometers are great for checking the surface areas of the grill, although they aren't designed to measure the internal temperatures of food. These thermometers allow you to take temperatures at a distance, from mere inches to a few feet away from the grill. Simply aim the laser at the grill grate, squeeze the trigger, and receive a reading in a matter of seconds. Check the temperature of the grill grate in a few spots, as different areas will be hotter than others. Yes, charcoal grills are fitted with built-in dial thermometers (usually in the cover), but I find that they can often be off by as much as 50°F! I'd rather not second-guess.

Grill Basket—A grill basket makes it easier to grill delicate vegetables like the Brussels sprouts in Charred Brussels Sprouts with Soft-Boiled Egg and Orange-Chili Glaze (page 67) and the shishito peppers in Singed Shishito Peppers with Sugar Snap Peas and Citrus Mango Salt (page 71), and cook carrots directly in the coals so they don't get lost (Coal-Roasted Carrots with Ricotta, Herbs, and Black Pepper Honey on page 138). Not to be confused with the hinged and handled variety used for turning fish, vegetable grill baskets are typically square or round, with an open top and small holes on the bottom to prevent food from falling through. They are inexpensive and widely available in kitchen stores and online.

Fire Starters—While you certainly can use a chimney starter or electric starter to light your charcoal grill, I don't personally find it necessary. Again, I'm a minimalist when it comes to specialty items. I simply build the coals at the base of the grill and light with fire starters and an Aim 'n Flame kitchen lighter. Fire starters are made of a mix of wood and wax and my favorite brands are Royal Oak tumbleweeds and Rutland Safe Lite squares because they ignite quickly, burn cleanly, and smell naturally fragrant. Whatever you do, *never* use lighter fluid to start your fire as it makes your food taste like chemicals.

Fireproof Gloves—This is not the item to skimp on quality! Well-made fire-proof gloves are indispensable when cooking with live fire. Choose gloves with long cuffs that are well-padded but still flexible. They should feel comfortable whether you are using tongs or handling a chef's knife. Fireproof gloves are mandatory when cooking food in the coals (see "In the Coals," page 128).

FIRING UP YOUR GRILL

The ritual of building and lighting the fire is the most primal and satisfying part of cooking outdoors, and sometimes it can be the most challenging. There are lots of opinions out there on how to set up a charcoal grill. I've found, in my many years of grilling, that cooking over an even bed of coals gives the best results.

Building Your Fire

To build your fire, it's best to scoop the charcoal rather than pouring directly from the bag to avoid any small wood shards and dust from clogging the grill vents. Putting the larger lump pieces on the bottom helps for a longer burn and doesn't block the vent holes or restrict airflow. Arrange the coals so they are mostly flat, three to four layers deep. Having a substantial amount of coals will keep your fire going for several hours without the need to replenish the coals. Even before you light the grill, make sure the bottom vents are open so that you have plenty of airflow, the fire needs oxygen to ignite and keep going. With the lid off, put four fire starters in the coals, one in the center and three around. Light the fire starters with an Aim n' Flame kitchen lighter. After

AVOIDING FLARE-UPS

Flare-ups usually happen because of meat with high fat content, or sauces and oily marinades dripping down off the food and hitting the burning coals—essentially causing a grease fire. Besides being a little scary, these bursts of intense flames can also incinerate your food to the point of no return. Flare-ups tend to occur soon after food is placed on the grill or once it's been flipped. A small flare-up (where the flames don't even reach the food) is expected here and there, especially with beef, and can actually add charred flavor to the food. To prevent more severe flare-ups, a good rule of thumb is to keep your grill clean and never to overcrowd the surface. If larger flare-ups occur (see Grilled Bone-In Prime Rib Eye, page 107), the best action is to immediately close the lid to cut the supply of oxygen and suffocate the flames. Wait and watch through the vents, and once you see the flare-up extinguished, it's safe to uncover. Another option is to carefully remove the food from the grill and onto a side platter and wait for the flare-up to subside. Either way, mastering the grill requires your full attention and you should always keep a close eye on whatever you're cooking and never walk away from burning coals.

you light the coals, allow them to burn for 10 to 15 minutes, until you see a nice fire going and some of the coals turning red. Carefully secure the top grate in place with gloves and tongs, cover with the lid, and open the top vent fully so that air properly circulates in the grill and smoke can escape. Leave the lid on for 10 to 15 minutes, until the flames die down and the coals start to ash over. Uncover the grill. Look at the beauty! Now you are ready to start cooking!

STAY SAFE

This may be the most important section in this book, so please read it thoroughly! Follow these guidelines for keeping yourself and your friends and family safe while cooking with fire.

· Never use your grill indoors or in a garage.

· Keep your grill well away from surrounding structures, such as your home, garage, fences, and patio railings. Don't put your grill under tree limbs or near brush either.

· Set up your grill only on a flat surface and make sure it is sturdy and can't be tipped over.

· Loose clothing can easily catch fire, so be sure your shirtsleeves or apron strings don't hang over the grill. I also advise wearing closed-toe shoes and avoid grilling barefoot or in flip-flops.

· Set up a "kid-free" zone and don't allow children (or pets) to play near the grill.

· Never leave a lit grill unattended or try to move it while hot. Remember, a charcoal grill will stay hot for several hours after use.

· Allow the coals to cool off completely before disposing of them, as well as the ash, in a metal container.

· Keep a fire extinguisher, a box of salt, or a box of baking soda in close proximity to your grilling area in case of emergency.

BASICS (SAUCES & RUBS)

Sometimes, just a sprinkle of great-quality sea salt and a few turns of freshly cracked black pepper are all you need seasoning-wise to bring live fire foods to life, but there are so many other spices out there that can take your outdoor cooking to an entirely new level. They're the essential seasonings that kick off your cookout and give fired foods their character, personality, and soul. The rubs and sauces in this chapter are building blocks of flavor for you to up the ante— basics that I treat as the foundation in many of the recipes in this book. There's no shortage of commercial rubs, marinades, and sauces on the market, and many will produce tasty barbecue. But if you want to truly express culinary creativity, it's best to make them yourself. So let's talk about some of these and how they can be used to enhance your charcoal experience.

The sauces in this chapter are our signature offerings at Charcoal, found on every table for guests to mix and match with their dishes as they wish. Several perform double duty and act as a marinade or will be brushed on the meat while it's grilling (see J1-Marinated Skirt Steak, page 104; Chimichurri-Marinated Hanger Steak, page 112; and Smoked and Grilled Bone-In Short Rib with Barbecue Sauce, page 213). Marinades and sauces add a punch of flavor. They tenderize the meat, which breaks down its fibers because they contain some type of acid like lemon juice, vinegar, or wine. Brush any of these sauces on your meats in the final stages of cooking to add color, shine and flavor. Don't be afraid to experiment and have fun!

My dry rubs are mixtures of salt, sugar, and spices, and they are one of the easiest ways to boost flavor and give pork, beef, fish, and even vegetables a crust when grilling. Be sure to use super-fresh spices (optimal potency is two to three months) when you make a spice rub and store it away from the hot stove.

Use these recipes as a jumping-off point and experiment at home making rubs with what you have in your cupboard to establish your personal flavor profile. Keep in mind that the balanced base of dry rubs always involves two of the oldest spices known to man—sugar and salt—and then build from there.

◇◇

J1 Steak Sauce

MAKES 3 CUPS

When I was a teenager, my buddies and I would skate over to a little café in Santa Monica for breakfast after working up an appetite from surfing. More often than not, my go-to order was steak and eggs; medium-rare and sunny-side up. Being a kid, naturally I'd drown my plate in A.1. Sauce, sopping up all the goodness with toasted sourdough. As a chef, I was determined to create my own homemade version, mimicking those nostalgic flavors but with more umami and salty tang. While it may seem like there are a lot of ingredients in this recipe, none of them are difficult to find. Super simple to make and far better than the commercially made stuff, this recipe yields a fair amount so you can always have it on hand; simply portion into individual containers and freeze a few. J1 makes a perfect marinade for grilled J1-Marinated Skirt Steak (page 104) or drizzled over eggs for breakfast.

1 cup ketchup

½ cup Dijon mustard

½ cup yellow mustard

½ cup golden raisins

¼ cup balsamic vinegar

¼ cup apple cider vinegar

½ cup freshly squeezed orange juice

1 cup Worcestershire sauce

½ cup packed dark brown sugar

5 white button mushrooms, wiped of grit and sliced

4 anchovy fillets, packed in oil and drained

3 garlic cloves, smashed after removing the germ (see Note)

2 shallots, sliced

¼ cup fresh tarragon leaves

1 tablespoon celery seeds

1 tablespoon fine sea salt

1 teaspoon freshly ground black pepper

½ teaspoon ground cloves

½ teaspoon ground cinnamon

½ teaspoon cayenne

1. Heat a large saucepan over medium-high heat. Place the ketchup, ½ cup water, the mustards, raisins, vinegars, orange juice, Worcestershire, and brown sugar in the heated saucepan. Stir with a wooden spoon to combine. Add the mushrooms, anchovies, garlic, shallots, tarragon, celery seeds, salt, black pepper, cloves, cinnamon, and cayenne. Mix well to incorporate. Bring the sauce to a boil, then reduce the heat to low. Gently simmer, uncovered, stirring occasionally to dissolve the brown sugar, until the sauce is reduced and slightly thickened, 20 to 25 minutes.

2. Working in batches if necessary, ladle the sauce into a blender, preferably a Vitamix, filling it no more than halfway. Puree on low speed for a few seconds, then increase to medium speed until the sauce is completely smooth. Be sure to hold down the lid with a kitchen towel for safety. Pour the sauce through a fine-mesh strainer into a heatproof bowl, pushing the solids with the back of a wooden spoon. Discard the solids. Repeat with the remaining sauce until completely blended and strained.

3. Transfer the sauce to a tightly covered bowl or individual jars/containers and refrigerate until ready to use. The sauce may be stored, covered, in the refrigerator for up to 2 weeks or frozen for up to 3 months.

Smoked Paprika Chimichurri
with Pickled Mustard Seeds

J1 Steak Sauce

Red Wine Chipotle
Barbecue Sauce

REMOVING GERM OF GARLIC

The green shoot in the center of
garlic cloves is known as the germ,
and it tends to give your dish a bitter
bite and burn at the end, which
can lead to indigestion. I always
remove it, but you can skip this step
throughout the recipes if you wish.
To remove the germ, simply cut the
garlic cloves in half and remove the
germ with a paring knife.

Smoked Paprika Chimichurri with Pickled Mustard Seeds

MAKES 2 CUPS

An essential part of Argentinean cuisine, a bowl of chimichurri can be found on every dinner table. This is one of the condiments we showcase at Charcoal, and I love the way the bright acidity of vinegar plays off the grassiness of fresh herbs. My backyard herb garden provided the inspiration for this classic sauce and from there I started playing around and mixing in other elements, like the pickled mustard seeds, which add a unique texture. The variations on this recipe are endless. Feel free to experiment and use whatever fresh herbs you have on hand. This colorful chimichurri sauce doubles as a marinade (Chimichurri-Marinated Hanger Steak, page 112; Chicken Salsa Verde, page 96; and Smoky Grilled Chicken Wings, page 211) and as an accompaniment to all cuts of beef. It also pairs wonderfully with mild seafood, such as halibut or Scallop Carpaccio with Chimichurri and Lemon Bread Crumbs (page 173).

2 cups packed fresh flat-leaf parsley leaves

1 cup packed wild arugula, stemmed

¾ cup packed fresh oregano leaves

¼ cup fresh thyme leaves

2 tablespoons fresh rosemary leaves

1 tablespoon fresh sage leaves

7 garlic cloves, coarsely chopped after removing the germ (see Note, page 31)

2 tablespoons Dijon mustard

2 tablespoons smoked paprika

2 teaspoons Piment d'Espelette (see Note, page 34) or cayenne

2 tablespoons fine sea salt, plus more to taste

3 tablespoons white wine vinegar

3 tablespoons Banyuls vinegar (see Note)

Juice of 1 lemon

¼ cup Pickled Mustard Seeds (recipe follows)

2 small shallots, minced

1 cup extra-virgin olive oil, preferably Arbequina

¼ cup lemon verbena or nasturtium leaves (optional), finely chopped

In the bowl of a food processor, combine the parsley, arugula, oregano, thyme, rosemary, sage, and garlic. Pulse until the herbs and garlic begin to break down—feel free to chop the herbs and garlic by hand if you prefer. Add the mustard, paprika, Piment d'Espelette, and salt. Pulse again to incorporate. Pour in the water, the vinegars, and the lemon juice. Puree briefly until the liquids are fully incorporated and the mixture is chunky. Scrape into a mixing bowl and stir in the pickled mustard seeds, shallots, and olive oil until combined. Season again with salt if necessary. Fold in the lemon verbena, if using. The chimichurri may be stored, covered, in the refrigerator for up to 1 week.

recipe continues

Pickled Mustard Seeds

MAKES ½ CUP

I love the pop of pickled mustard seeds. Plump, sweet, and sour, with a caviar-like texture that begs to be popped, one by one, between your teeth. A spoonful of pickled mustard seeds adds zip to sauces and vinaigrettes and makes a great condiment for a charcuterie and cheese board.

½ cup yellow or brown mustard seeds (or a mixture of both)

1 cup Champagne vinegar

1 cup sparkling wine, such as Cava or Prosecco

Put the mustard seeds in a small container or jar with a lid and pour in ½ cup of the vinegar and ½ cup of the wine (enjoy the rest of the bottle). Tightly cover the container and store in the refrigerator for 5 days. Strain and discard the liquid. Transfer the soaked mustard seeds to a small saucepan and pour in the remaining ½ cup vinegar and ½ cup wine. Bring to a boil over medium heat. Reduce the heat to medium-low and simmer until the mustard seeds swell and nearly double in size, 5 to 7 minutes. Remove from the heat and let cool. Pour the mustard seeds, along with the liquid, into a covered container and store in the refrigerator for up to 2 weeks.

Red Wine Chipotle Barbecue Sauce

MAKES 1 QUART

Homemade barbecue sauce is an essential staple for outdoor cooking and I always have some on hand at Charcoal—and in my refrigerator at home. Chipotle is the secret weapon in this simple barbecue sauce, which goes beautifully with pork, chicken, beef, and all types of ribs (see Smoked Lamb Ribs with Fermented Black Beans and Charred Scallion Vinaigrette, page 205). Rich with the complexity and depth of red wine and subtly flavored with smoked paprika and spicy ancho chilies, this tangy tomato-based barbecue sauce (sans ketchup) is infinitely better than the overly sweet bottled stuff. Plus, you can enjoy the rest of the bottle of wine with dinner.

2 tablespoons grapeseed oil

1 medium onion, diced small

2 garlic cloves, chopped after removing the germ (see Note, page 31)

Fine sea salt

½ cup (4 ounces) tomato paste

1½ cups dry red wine, such as Cabernet Sauvignon

1¼ cups balsamic vinegar

One 28-ounce can diced tomatoes, with juice

1 cup packed dark brown sugar

1 chipotle in adobo sauce, chopped

1 ancho chili pepper, stemmed and seeded

2 teaspoons smoked paprika

1 bay leaf, preferably fresh

1. Heat a saucepan over medium heat and coat with the grapeseed oil. Add the onion and garlic and season with salt. Cook while stirring until fragrant and just golden in color, about 2 minutes. Stir in the tomato paste until it is fully incorporated and begins to melt into the onions, taking care to stir often to prevent burning. This should take 3 to 4 minutes. Deglaze with the wine and cook until reduced by half, about 5 minutes.

2. Add the vinegar, tomatoes, brown sugar, chipotle, ancho chili, smoked paprika, and bay leaf, stirring to incorporate. Bring the sauce to a boil, then reduce the heat to low. Gently simmer, uncovered, stirring periodically to prevent scorching, until the sauce is reduced and slightly thickened, about 1 hour. Remove and discard the bay leaf.

3. Working in batches if necessary, ladle the sauce into a blender, preferably a Vitamix, filling it no more than halfway. Puree on low speed for a few seconds, then increase to medium speed until the sauce is completely smooth. Be sure to hold down the lid with a kitchen towel for safety. Pour the sauce through a fine-mesh strainer into a heatproof bowl, pushing the solids with the back of a wooden spoon. Discard the solid pieces. Repeat with the remaining sauce until completely blended and strained.

4. Transfer the sauce to a bowl or individual jars/containers and tightly cover. Refrigerate until ready to use. The sauce may be stored, covered, in the refrigerator for up to 10 days or frozen for up to 3 months.

Basque Vinegar

MAKES 1 QUART

After I graduated from Santa Monica High School, I packed up and moved to Paris to embark on my culinary career and learn the art and rigor of traditional French cuisine. I landed a job in the kitchen of one of the best fine-dining restaurants in the city, and like most places in Paris, the restaurant closed during the month of August for vacation. I took a surfing trip down to Biarritz in the Basque region of Southwest France, famous for its beautiful, sandy beach and big waves. A friend of mine, who was a local, took me to a great little tapas bar called La Tantina de Burgos. They had a bottle of this incredible infused vinegar on every table and I fell in love with the elevated flavors. A perfect condiment to cut the richness of steak and fatty meats, my version can now be found on every table at Charcoal. Serve with your favorite meat in small side bowls for dipping, as a salad dressing, or in place of plain vinegar in recipes. You'll see this recipe utilized throughout the book, such as in Oysters with Shallots and Basque Vinegar (page 86) and Smoky Grilled Chicken Wings (page 211).

1 tablespoon whole black peppercorns

1 tablespoon whole fennel seeds

1 tablespoon whole coriander seeds

4 fresh thyme sprigs

2 fresh rosemary sprigs

2 bay leaves, preferably fresh

3 garlic cloves, skin on

2 small shallots, peeled and quartered

1 small lemongrass stalk, tough outer layer removed and smashed

1 small carrot, cut into thin strips

One 1-inch piece fresh ginger, peeled and cut into thin strips

1 dried red chili, such as chile de arbol (see Note)

2½ cups distilled white vinegar

1. Heat a dry sauté pan over low heat. Place the peppercorns, fennel, and coriander in the pan. Toast until fragrant, shaking the pan periodically to prevent scorching, about 5 minutes.

2. Transfer the toasted spices to a glass bottle with a spout (I like to use a recycled whiskey bottle). Add the thyme, rosemary, bay leaves, garlic, shallots, lemongrass, carrot, ginger, and chili—if they don't fit down the neck of the bottle, cut them down a little smaller. Pour in the vinegar and ½ cup water. Secure the spout and set aside at room temperature for 3 to 5 days to infuse the vinegar with the aromatics. The flavor will become stronger as it sits. After using, refill with vinegar to keep the aromatics submerged. The vinegar may be stored, covered, in the refrigerator for up to 6 months.

Ingredient Note: Chile de Arbol
Chile de arbol are small dried red chilies that have about the same heat level as cayenne, which may be used as a substitute.

Jefferson's
Reserve

Groth Reserve Cask Finish

Extra matured in French
Oak casks which
previously held Groth
Cabernet Sauvignon.

MASTER BLENDER

Very Old
Kentucky Straight Bourbon Whiskey
Very Small Batch

45.1% Alc./Vol. (90.2 Proof) • 750 ML

Charcoal Ketchup

MAKES 1 QUART

I'm fairly confident that just about every home in America has a bottle of ketchup somewhere in the refrigerator. Sure, grabbing the store-bought bottle is easier, but I wouldn't be telling you to make your own ketchup if the taste wasn't worth it; it has more flavor, more texture, and there's no corn syrup. Plus, you can tell people this is your own, homemade, secret recipe and get bragging rights. I won't tell. You can make this recipe in under an hour from start to finish with basic cooking equipment, so as long as you feel comfortable with simmering and stirring, you can be an expert ketchup maker. Feel free to tweak the spices to suit your own tastes.

½ teaspoon smoked paprika

½ teaspoon ground mustard

½ teaspoon ground cumin

½ teaspoon ground coriander

¼ teaspoon ground cloves

¼ teaspoon ground cinnamon

¼ teaspoon ground allspice

¼ teaspoon ground ginger

2 tablespoons grapeseed oil

1 medium onion, halved and sliced ½ inch thick

5 garlic cloves, smashed after removing the germ (see Note, page 31)

Fine sea salt

Two 6-ounce cans tomato paste

One 28-ounce can whole tomatoes, with juice

One 14½-ounce can whole tomatoes, with juice

½ cup red wine vinegar

2 tablespoons Tabasco sauce

2 tablespoons non-pareil capers, drained

5 tablespoons packed dark brown sugar

¼ teaspoon dried oregano

Freshly ground black pepper

Juice of 1 lemon

1. Heat a dry sauté pan over medium-low heat. Place the spices in the pan and toast, shaking the pan periodically to prevent scorching, until fragrant, about 5 minutes. Set aside.

2. Heat a 3-quart saucepan over medium heat and coat with the grapeseed oil. Add the onion and garlic and season with salt. Cook and stir until well caramelized, 5 to 7 minutes. Stir in the tomato paste until it is fully incorporated and begins to melt into the onion, taking care to stir often to prevent from burning. Reduce the heat to low and stir in the reserved toasted spices.

3. Add all of the canned tomatoes, vinegar, Tabasco, and capers. Cook, stirring to incorporate, for 2 minutes. Sprinkle in the brown sugar, oregano, and pepper. Raise the heat to medium-high and bring to a simmer. Cook, stirring occasionally, until thick and glossy, about 30 minutes.

4. Working in batches if necessary, ladle the ketchup into a blender, preferably a Vitamix, filling it no more than halfway. Puree on low speed for a few seconds, then increase to medium speed until the ketchup is completely smooth. Be sure to hold down the lid with a kitchen towel for safety. Squeeze in the lemon juice and season with salt and pepper if needed.

5. Pour the ketchup through a fine-mesh strainer into a heatproof bowl, pushing the solids with the back of a wooden spoon. Discard the solids. Repeat with the remaining sauce until completely blended and strained. Cool immediately over a bowl of ice. The ketchup may be stored, covered, in the refrigerator for up to 3 weeks or frozen for up to 3 months.

California Chili Sauce

MAKES 2 CUPS

When I set out to reimagine the piquant rooster sauce, Sriracha, I ended up developing something that hit the right spicy, garlicky notes but had a brighter, fresher, and fruitier flavor. The key to Sriracha is the fermentation process, which strikes a delicate balance between funky and robust. Comparable in size, flavor, and heat to a red jalapeño, Fresno chilies hail from my home state of California and impart a subtle smokiness to this sauce. Just about everything tastes more vibrant with a dose of this condiment—stir it into mayo or sour cream, or add a few dashes to deviled eggs, chicken wings, chili, or mac-n-cheese.

1 pound red Fresno chili peppers, stems removed and caps intact

½ cup packed light brown sugar

6 garlic cloves, smashed after removing the germ (see Note, page 31)

1 tablespoon fine sea salt

½ cup distilled white vinegar

1. Put the chili peppers in the bowl of a food processor and add the brown sugar, garlic, and salt. Pulse until coarsely combined and chunky, about 1 minute.

2. Transfer the chili mixture to a large sealable glass jar and cover with a couple layers of cheesecloth. Set aside at room temperature until it begins to bubble and ferment, 2 to 3 days. It is important to put the top on the jar and shake the chili mixture daily to keep it from separating. Remove the lid and re-cover with cheesecloth after shaking.

3. Once the chili mixture is fermented, place it in a blender, preferably a Vitamix, and pour in the vinegar. Blend on medium speed until the vinegar is fully incorporated and the consistency is completely smooth.

4. Pour the chili sauce into a saucepan and bring to a boil over medium-high heat. Once it comes to a boil, reduce the heat to low and gently simmer, uncovered and stirring periodically, until slightly thickened, about 10 minutes. Cool completely.

5. Transfer the sauce to a bowl or individual jars/containers and tightly cover. Refrigerate until ready to use. The sauce may be stored, covered, in the refrigerator for up to 1 month or frozen for up to 3 months.

Hibiscus Flower Rub

MAKES 1 CUP

Reminiscent of cranberries and pomegranate in their tartness and color, hibiscus are dried deep red–violet flowers with a tangy, berry-like flavor. Also called Jamaica in Spanish, hibiscus is a beloved *agua fresca* beverage featured in taquerias and Latin markets (where it is often sold in bags with other spices and herbs). The floral fruitiness of hibiscus is well balanced by the assertive, yet nuanced, variety of peppercorns. This rub is exceptional on fish (see Cedar Plank Salmon with Hibiscus, page 202), but also brightens the flavor of snapper, scallops, and lobster.

10 Javanese long peppers (see Note)

1 tablespoon whole black peppercorns

2 teaspoons whole pink peppercorns

1 teaspoon whole green peppercorns

½ cup dried hibiscus flowers

¼ cup packed light brown sugar

3 tablespoons fine sea salt

2 teaspoons sweet paprika

1 teaspoon Piment d'Espelette (see Note, page 34) or cayenne

1. Heat a dry sauté pan over medium-low heat and add the Javanese peppers and all the peppercorns. Toast until fragrant, shaking the pan periodically to prevent scorching, about 5 minutes. Spoon the toasted peppercorns into a clean spice grinder or coffee mill. Add the hibiscus flowers. Grind until the mixture is a semi-coarse powder.

2. Pour the pepper mixture into a small mixing bowl. Add the brown sugar, salt, paprika, and Piment d'Espelette. Stir to fully incorporate and distribute the ingredients. This may be stored in a covered container at room temperature (away from the heat of the stove) for up to 3 months.

Ingredient Note: Javanese Long Pepper
Also known as Indonesian long pepper, these long, pine cone–looking peppercorns have a complex flavor all their own. Their warm, fruity-musky aroma has hints of nutmeg and cinnamon without being overly spicy. The Javanese long pepper's distinctive, floral quality is the perfect counterpoint to hibiscus flowers and elevates this rub into something extra special. You can find them in gourmet markets or online.

Sweet and Hot Seafood Rub with Jalapeño

MAKES ABOUT ½ CUP

Most rubs you'll come across are best suited for barbecuing meat and just too heavy for fish. But I was determined to develop one to enhance the flavor of grilled seafood. This spice and herb mixture strikes the right chord of sweet and spicy without being overpowering. Massaging the seasonings into the exterior of fish infuses the flesh with flavor and creates a crisp coating to add texture. An easy way to give a simple piece of fish an extra punch, this rub works extremely well on thick, meaty seafood such as swordfish, arctic char, tuna, and shrimp.

¼ cup packed dark
  brown sugar

3 tablespoons jalapeño
  powder

1 teaspoon ground sansho
  pepper (see Note)

1 teaspoon smoked
  paprika

1 teaspoon dried oregano

1 teaspoon celery seeds

1 teaspoon fine sea salt

½ teaspoon ground
  coriander

½ teaspoon granulated
  garlic

In a mixing bowl, combine the brown sugar, jalapeño powder, sansho pepper, paprika, oregano, celery seeds, salt, coriander, and garlic. Mix well with a spoon to distribute the ingredients evenly. Transfer to a glass jar or container with a tight-fitting lid and store at room temperature (away from the heat of the stove) for up to 3 months.

Ingredient Note: Sansho Pepper
These little Japanese green peppercorns impart a vibrant, citrusy flavor to this rub, without overwhelming the delicate flavors of seafood. While not technically in the pepper family, these tangy, slightly spicy berries can be found ground or whole in Asian markets or online. S&B is a leading brand most commonly distributed.

Lemon Pepper

MAKES ½ CUP

Lemon pepper was one of my mother's favorite pantry staples. She'd keep it in a shaker and come dinnertime, she'd often whip it out from the cupboard and sprinkle it on almost everything for a flavor boost. Lemon pepper is great to have on hand to add tang and spice to chicken, fish, meat, or vegetables without adding fat. It's also a key ingredient in Mom's Honey Chicken (page 99), naturally. Forget the store-bought version in the spice aisle and take a little bit of time to make this fresh, homemade recipe.

1 teaspoon whole black peppercorns

1 teaspoon whole fennel seeds

1 teaspoon whole coriander seeds

¼ cup dried lemon peel

1 tablespoon packed dark brown sugar

2 teaspoons food-grade citric acid

½ teaspoon fine sea salt

¼ teaspoon granulated onion

¼ teaspoon granulated garlic

¼ teaspoon ground sansho pepper (see Note, page 44)

Heat a small, dry skillet over low heat and add the peppercorns, fennel, and coriander. Combine and toast for just 1 minute to release the fragrant oils, shaking the pan so the spices don't scorch. Remove and place in a spice mill or clean coffee grinder. Grind the toasted spices together for a few seconds until they are broken down but still a bit chunky (make sure you thoroughly wipe out your coffee grinder before you make coffee again). Pour the spices into a small mixing bowl and add the lemon peel, brown sugar, citric acid, salt, onion, garlic, and sansho pepper. Mix well with a spoon to distribute the ingredients evenly. Transfer to a glass jar or container with a tight-fitting lid and store at room temperature (away from the heat of the stove) for up to 3 months.

Fermented Black Bean Rub

MAKES ABOUT 2 CUPS

Fermented black beans are like an assertive soy sauce, with pungent flavor that lingers in a musky-funky space. I was first exposed to these salty black jewels when I worked with Wolfgang Puck at Chinois on Main in the early '90s, and I've been playing around with them ever since. Here, the fermented black beans are oven-dried to concentrate their flavor, and then ground into a spice powder. This charcoal-colored rub is integral to the Smoked Lamb Ribs with Fermented Black Beans and Charred Scallion Vinaigrette (page 205), and also adds pop when added to ground beef mixture for burgers or meat loaf (just omit the brown sugar in the recipe).

½ cup fermented black beans (see Note)

½ cup packed light brown sugar

⅓ cup fine sea salt

⅓ cup freshly ground black pepper

⅓ cup smoked paprika

1. Preheat the oven to 200°F. Line a rimmed baking sheet with parchment paper.

2. Spread the fermented black beans evenly over the prepared baking sheet and bake, shaking the pan periodically, until the beans are dry to the touch, about 1 hour. Set aside to cool. Transfer the beans to a clean spice mill or coffee grinder. Grind into a fine powder. Pour the black bean powder into a mixing bowl and add the brown sugar, salt, pepper, and paprika. Mix well with a spoon to distribute the ingredients evenly. Transfer to a glass jar or container with a tight-fitting lid and store at room temperature (away from the heat of the stove) for up to 3 months.

Ingredient Note: Fermented Black Beans
These are not the black beans you find in Mexican cooking but, in fact, black soybeans—the same as in miso and soy sauce. Dried and fermented with salt, the process turns the beans soft, savory, umami-tasting, and delicious. A staple in Chinese cuisine, the most common way to cook with fermented black beans is in a stir-fry. Here, I like to dry them out and grind them into a powder to impart a sweet, funky aroma. Fermented black beans are typically sold at Asian markets in plastic bags.

Dried Porcini Rub

MAKES ABOUT ½ CUP

Porcini, the Italian mushrooms prized for their meaty texture and heady aroma, have an earthy sweetness when fresh and an intense muskiness when dried. Dried porcini mushrooms are thankfully widely available and significantly less expensive than fresh. In ground form, these magic mushrooms add an immeasurable umami-packed magnitude to this rub, making it rich and delicious. The brown sugar in the mix brings back some of the natural sweetness found in fresh porcini that is often lost in the drying process, and also helps develop the char and create a "steak house" caramelized crust on meat. The red pepper flakes provide a bit of heat for those who like it hot. This is a darkly colored spice rub that can make the meat look like it's burned, so keep that in mind when cooking. You can use it on all types of steak, such as filet mignon and prime rib, but it lends an especially sophisticated flavor to Porcini-Dusted New York Strip (page 111).

1 ounce dried porcini mushrooms

1 tablespoon whole black peppercorns

3 tablespoons packed dark brown sugar

2 teaspoons dried red pepper flakes

1 teaspoon dried thyme

1 teaspoon fine sea salt

Place the porcini mushrooms and peppercorns in a clean spice mill or coffee grinder. Grind into a fine powder. Pour the mushroom-pepper powder into a small mixing bowl. Add the brown sugar, red pepper flakes, thyme, and salt. Stir to fully incorporate and distribute the ingredients. Store at room temperature in a covered container (away from the heat of the stove) for up to 3 months.

Black Sage Rub

MAKES ABOUT ½ CUP

The highly aromatic, piney-woody essence of sage is a perfect counterpoint to the subtle smokiness of activated charcoal. Striking in color and bold in flavor, this savory rub uses only a handful of ingredients and is exceptional with all types of poultry (especially turkey), as well as lamb and pork. Try it sprinkled on your favorite roasted butternut squash at your next holiday dinner.

2 tablespoons dried sage powder

2 tablespoons packed light brown sugar

2 tablespoons fine sea salt

1 tablespoon activated charcoal (see Note)

1 teaspoon Piment d'Espelette (see Note, page 34) or cayenne

1 teaspoon smoked paprika

In a small mixing bowl, combine the sage, brown sugar, salt, activated charcoal, Piment d'Espelette, and paprika. Mix well to distribute the ingredients evenly. Transfer to a glass jar or container with a tight-fitting lid and store at room temperature (away from the heat of the stove) for up to 3 months.

Ingredient Note: Activated Charcoal
Used as a detoxifier and in Instagram-worthy recipes, activated charcoal is typically the by-product of burning coconut shells or hardwood to extremely high temperatures until completely burned into a powder. A natural purifier, food-grade activated charcoal has an earthy, slightly smoky taste and jet-black hue. You can purchase food-grade charcoal powder at health food stores, in fine food stores, or online.

Coffee Rub

MAKES ABOUT ½ CUP

This earthy coffee-based rub sings with notes of orange, vanilla, and cardamom for a bold, well-rounded flavor. The dark and toasty undertone of this coffee-based rub jazzes up anything you want to cook up quickly on the grill, and pairs particularly well with rich meats, such as brisket, sirloin, all types of ribs, and Grilled Lamb Chops with Charred Eggplant Puree (page 121). For a vegetable alternative, sprinkle the rub over oven-roasted parsnips in the last five minutes of cooking to add an extra kick. This recipe is quick to make, and you can double, triple, or quadruple it easily.

2 tablespoons packed light brown sugar

2 whole vanilla beans, split and scraped

3 tablespoons finely ground coffee, preferably arabica

2 tablespoons dried, ground orange peel

2 tablespoons fine sea salt

2 teaspoons ground cardamom

In a medium mixing bowl, combine the brown sugar and vanilla bean seeds. Add the coffee, orange peel, salt, and cardamom. Stir to fully incorporate and distribute the ingredients. Store at room temperature in a covered container (away from the heat of the stove) for up to 3 months.

OVER THE COALS

I'm a firm believer that grilling brings people together. Much like carving the holiday turkey, the ritual is typically deemed a man's job and has an innate sense of communal gathering and loving family. One of my earliest memories growing up was hanging out at my neighbor's house for Sunday barbecue after Little League games and watching my friend's dad, Frank Jimenez, tend to the grill with a Miller Lite beer in one hand and a king-size spatula in the other. Frank brought the neighborhood together with his grill. To this day, when I get a whiff of drifting smoke from someone grilling in a yard nearby, the smell triggers fond memories and takes me back to way back when. Grilling is about summertime and cooking outdoors; grilling is also fundamentally about time and attention.

I'm not one to overcomplicate the marriage of food and fire, so I keep it simple by relying on only direct heat grilling, instead of setting up two hot and cool heat zones. Two-zone grilling is when you set up two areas of your grill by piling more coals on one side of the grill (high direct heat), and then fewer coals on the other side (low indirect heat). The hotter side is typically preferred for searing thinner cuts of meat, such as skinless, boneless chicken breasts and flank steak, while the cooler side is preferred for cooking larger cuts of meat without burning the exterior before the center is cooked, such as pork shoulder, or to finish cooking meats after searing on the hot, direct side. Honestly, I find a simple, even hot zone throughout the grill perfectly fine. What I do encourage is to turn the meat often and rest it periodically to prevent the outside from burning, and control the internal temperature from getting too hot and potentially overcooking. So basically, by constantly flipping the meat and taking it off the grill to rest, it has the same effect as indirect cooking. I'd rather harness the flame of the coals by opening and closing the air vents and lid, to avoid flare-ups and to keep the cooking temperature constant. Working the vents allows *you* to control the airflow and subsequent heat, and not the other way around! Plus, grills come in various sizes and it's often challenging to set up two-zone cooking areas in an everyday Weber kettle grill, for example, that is only eighteen to twenty-two inches in diameter; there is simply not ample space to achieve the direct/indirect cooking method successfully, in my opinion. One-zone direct heat cooking does require you to mind the grill a bit more, but that's part of the grilling experience!

Grilling over direct heat and constantly flipping what you're grilling moreover creates a lot more flavor due to the meat juices and fat drippings trickling onto the hot coals to produce epic, aromatic steam, as the vapors rise and are reabsorbed into the meat to keep it moist. The grilling temperatures in this chapter range from 350°F (Mom's Honey Chicken, page 99), on up to very high heat of 700°F (Grilled Calamari with Blue Lake Green Beans, Almonds, and Lemon Bread Crumbs, page 89), so take care to read the recipes before getting the fire going. Remember: To increase the temperature, open the vents to let in more oxygen. To decrease the temperature, close the vents—but not completely, or the fire will go out!

Remember to always keep your grill grate clean by using a dry grill brush to scrape off any charred bits stuck to it. When getting ready to grill, many of the recipes require you rub the grill grate with oil when hot to create a nonstick surface.

Cooking on a grill adds an unsurpassed smoked, charred depth not only to meat but also to everyday breakfast, (Huevos Rancheros and Grilled Quesadilla with Tomatillo Sauce, page 59) and it transforms ordinary vegetables into something especially unexpected Grilled Chopped Vegetable Salad with Havarti, Bacon, Kalamata Olives, and Jo-Jo's Vinaigrette (page 61). While you can execute all of the recipes in this chapter on a gas grill (skip the coal instructions and just set the heat to the temperature specified in the instructions), you will sadly miss out on the charred, smoky effects only charcoal can offer.

GETTING YOUR GRILL GAME ON

When building a fire for your charcoal grill, I recommend using an ample amount of natural hardwood lump charcoal so you don't risk the coals dying out during the cook, filling your grill halfway up from the bottom to the top grate. I prefer a hickory and oak mix, and always organic when possible. You want an even layer of coals all the way to the diameter of the grill, so be sure to spread them out. Before you even light your grill, make sure to open the vents. The fire will need oxygen to keep going. To light the grill, I'm a fan of natural fire starter sticks; they're inexpensive and easy to use with no special chimney starter required (although you may use one if so inclined). With the lid off, stick four fire starters in the charcoal with one in the center and the other three around and light them with a kitchen lighter. After you light the coals, allow them to burn for about 10 to 15 minutes until you see a nice fire going and some of the coals turning red. Check to see if the coals are glowing evenly. If not, rake with a large grilling spatula and mix them around so that the dormant coals catch fire. Carefully secure the top grate in place with gloves and tongs, cover with the lid, and open the top vent fully so air properly circulates in the grill and smoke can escape. Leave the lid on for 10 to 15 minutes until the flames die down and the coals start to ash over. Uncover the grill and get ready to cook.

ADDING WOOD TO THE COALS

Charcoal gives you high, dry heat, but it doesn't impart much flavor. I like having subtle hints of wood flavor in my cooking but find it overpowering to strictly grill over wood alone. So, I combine the best of both worlds and often add a few wood chunks to the coals when grilling. When building your fire, simply add 5 to 7 chunks of unsoaked applewood, oak, or hickory and mix them into your coals so they burn evenly with the charcoal.

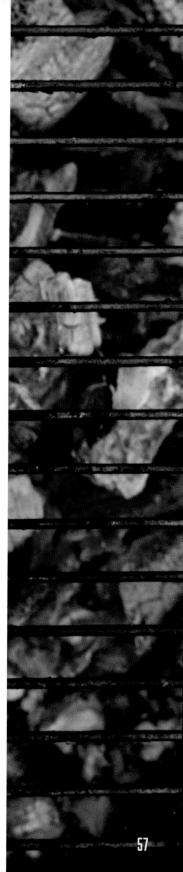

Huevos Rancheros and Grilled Quesadilla with Tomatillo Sauce

SERVES 4

I've lived here my whole life and Southern California, Los Angeles especially, has some of the best Mexican food in the country, hands down. Huevos rancheros and quesadillas are menu staples throughout the city, and when I go out to eat, it's usually a toss-up of which one I'll order. Truthfully, 90 percent of the time I get them both. To experience the best of both worlds, I morphed them together into one awesome Mexican dish. Ranchero, by definition, is typically a red sauce, but I prefer the tart tang of green tomatillo salsa verde to liven up the eggs and black beans. If you like, pick up a container of fresh pico de gallo sauce to serve on the side. Ideal for brunch, this recipe is simple enough to double if you're hosting a gathering.

2 tablespoons vegetable oil or bacon fat

½ sweet onion, finely diced

1 jalapeño, stemmed, halved, seeded, and minced

One 15½-ounce can black beans, drained and rinsed

½ cup vegetable stock

6 fresh cilantro sprigs, plus more, chopped, for garnish

Juice of 1 lime

¼ teaspoon fine sea salt

2 large poblano peppers

Eight 6-inch corn tortillas

2 cups shredded Mexican cheese blend

8 large eggs, preferably organic and free-range, cooked to your liking (scrambled, fried, or poached)

Tomatillo Sauce (recipe follows), warm

¼ cup crumbled Cotija cheese

1. Coat a small saucepan with the vegetable oil and place over medium heat. Add the onion and cook, stirring, until translucent, about 2 minutes. Add the jalapeño and continue to cook and stir until slightly softened, about 1 minute. Add the black beans, along with the stock. Bring to a simmer, stirring occasionally to prevent the beans from sticking, 8 to 10 minutes. Stir in the cilantro, lime juice, and salt. Cover and keep warm over very low heat.

2. Preheat a charcoal or gas grill to high heat (500°F).

3. Take a few paper towels and fold them several times to make a thick square. Blot a small amount of oil on the paper towel, then carefully and quickly wipe the hot grates of the grill. This will create a nonstick grilling surface. Put the poblanos on the hot grill until blistered and blackened on all sides, about 8 minutes. Put them in a bowl, cover with plastic wrap, and let sweat for about 10 minutes to loosen the

recipe continues

skins. Peel and rub off the charred skins. Split the poblanos in half and remove the cores and seeds. Cut into small pieces and set aside. You should have about ½ cup.

4. Lay 4 tortillas on a flat surface and divide an equal amount of shredded cheese and poblanos on top of each. Set the remaining 4 tortillas on top to enclose them like a sandwich. Transfer the tortillas to the hot grill and cook for 2 to 3 minutes on each side, until the cheese is melted and the tortillas are slightly charred. Remove from the grill and cover to keep warm.

5. Prepare the eggs as you wish.

6. To serve, put the quesadilla on four plates, spoon the black beans over, then lay the eggs on top. Pour the tomatillo sauce over the top and garnish with the Cotija and chopped cilantro.

Tomatillo Sauce

MAKES 1½ CUPS

Completely different from regular tomatoes, tomatillos have an addictive acidic tang that adds brightness to any Mexican-inspired meal, such as tacos. Be sure to remove the tomatillo's paper husk and rinse off any sticky residue before using. To enhance them with a bit more smoked flavor, you can rub the tomatillos with oil and grill them until they are softened and slightly charred before blending them with the other ingredients.

8 tomatillos (about 1 pound), husked, rinsed, and quartered

1 bunch fresh cilantro, tops ripped off

1 Hass avocado, halved, pitted, peeled, and coarsely chopped

2 garlic cloves, germ removed (see Note, page 31)

½ jalapeño, stemmed, halved, seeded, and chopped

1½ teaspoons sugar

¼ cup vegetable oil or bacon fat

½ teaspoon fine sea salt

1. In a blender, preferably a Vitamix, combine the tomatillos, ½ cup cilantro, avocado, garlic, jalapeño, and sugar. Blend until completely smooth and work in batches if necessary.

2. Heat a 2-quart saucepan over medium-high heat and coat with the oil. Add the tomatillo puree and whisk rapidly; it may bubble a bit. Reduce the heat to medium and simmer, whisking occasionally, until the sauce is slightly thickened and the raw tomatillo flavor is gone, 10 to 15 minutes. Season with the salt. Cover, reduce the heat to very low, and keep warm. You can prepare this up to 2 days in advance and store it, covered, in the refrigerator. Warm the sauce before using.

Grilled Chopped Vegetable Salad with Havarti, Bacon, Kalamata Olives, and Jo-Jo's Vinaigrette

SERVES 4 TO 6

My grilled rendition of this quintessential summer salad is loaded with so many goodies! It's chock-full of bright flavors and colors and an addictive variety of crunchy textures, and the charred vegetables take it to another level. The key to making a killer chopped salad is cutting all of the ingredients into a fairly uniform size, so you get all of the flavors in one perfect bite. In fact, I often eat this salad with a spoon instead of a fork to be sure I taste everything together.

Since the salad is served chilled, you can easily grill the vegetables a day before you plan to serve it. Not only does this make a fabulous side to any of the barbecued meats in this book, but it also shines as one of the all-time great entrée salads when you want a lighter meal. I use my favorite vegetables in this recipe, but you can certainly substitute what you like better or what looks good at the farmer's market.

1 sweet onion, sliced into ½-inch rounds

1 portobello mushroom cap, wiped of grit

¼ cup balsamic vinegar

¼ cup extra-virgin olive oil

Fine sea salt

1 celery stalk, ends trimmed

1 Persian cucumber

1 small zucchini, halved lengthwise

1 small yellow squash, halved lengthwise

½ pound green beans, preferably Blue Lake, ends trimmed

8 bacon strips, cut into thirds

1 romaine lettuce heart, quartered and cut crosswise into ¼-inch-thick strips

¼ head iceberg lettuce, cored, halved lengthwise and cut crosswise into ¼-inch-thick pieces

1 pint cherry tomatoes, halved lengthwise

6 ounces aged or firm Havarti cheese, diced (about ½ cup)

¼ cup kalamata olives, pitted and halved lengthwise

½ cup Jo-Jo's Vinaigrette (recipe follows)

Juice of ½ lemon

Freshly ground black pepper

1. Lay the onion rounds and mushroom flat on a rimmed baking sheet, drizzle with the vinegar and 2 tablespoons of the oil, and season with salt. You want to handle them separately so that the rings don't come apart and fall into the grill. Set aside for 15 minutes to let marinate. Rub the celery, cucumber, zucchini, and squash with the remaining 2 tablespoons oil to lightly coat. Season generously with salt.

2. Preheat a charcoal or gas grill to medium-high heat (400 to 450°F).

3. Working in batches, place the celery, cucumber, zucchini, squash, onion rounds, and mushroom on the grill and cook, turning periodically, until tender and lightly charred on all sides. Each vegetable takes a different amount of time, anywhere from 2 to 10 minutes. Transfer the vegetables to a side platter as they become

recipe continues

done. Cover and refrigerate the grilled vegetables for at least 1 hour to chill them. You may prepare the vegetables up to 1 day before you plan to serve the salad.

4. Bring a large pot of well-salted water to a boil over high heat. Prepare an ice bath by filling a large bowl halfway with water and adding a tray of ice cubes. Set a colander or mesh strainer inside the bowl of ice water and set aside.

5. Blanch the green beans until tender when pierced with a knife, about 2 minutes.

6. Use a slotted spoon or tongs to remove the green beans from the boiling water and plunge them into the colander to "shock" them (this stops the cooking process, cools them down right away, and locks in the bright green color). Once completely cool, pull out the colander or

strainer to drain. Pat the green beans dry with paper towels, cut into thirds, and set aside. The green beans can easily be prepared in advance, covered, and refrigerated for up to 1 day before you plan to serve the salad.

7. Heat a 10-inch sauté pan over medium heat and add the bacon pieces. Cook, stirring, until the bacon is fried and crispy, about 5 minutes. Transfer the bacon to a paper towel–lined plate to drain.

8. To serve, place the romaine and iceberg lettuce in a large salad bowl. Chop the grilled vegetables into small uniform pieces and add to the salad bowl. Add the green beans, bacon, tomatoes, Havarti, and olives. Toss well to distribute the ingredients evenly. Pour in the vinaigrette and lemon juice and toss again until well coated. Season with 6 turns of a peppermill.

Jo-Jo's Vinaigrette
MAKES ABOUT 2 CUPS

This French-style vinaigrette should always be in your refrigerator door. Thankfully, you will have plenty left over when you make this for the grilled chopped salad. Good on just about everything from sliced avocado to any variety of greens, this vinaigrette has just the right amount of acidity to complement the earthy depth of vegetables. For fun, I named this vinaigrette "Jo-Jo's"—it's a clever mashup of my name and Charcoal's Chef de Cuisine Joe Johnson.

1 tablespoon Dijon mustard

1 garlic clove, smashed with a back of a knife into a paste after removing the germ (see Note, page 31)

½ small shallot, finely chopped

Freshly ground black pepper

1 teaspoon fine sea salt

¼ cup balsamic vinegar

¼ cup apple cider vinegar

2 tablespoons red wine vinegar

1 cup grapeseed oil

½ cup extra-virgin olive oil

Juice of ½ lemon

In a large jar or container with a tight-fitting lid, combine the mustard, garlic, shallot, 6 turns of a peppermill, and salt (adding salt to the base of the vinaigrette before the oil is key so it dissolves). Pour in the vinegars and ¼ cup water. Pour in the grapeseed oil. Secure the lid and shake until the oil is incorporated. Add the olive oil and lemon juice. Shake again until the vinaigrette is fully emulsified. The vinaigrette keeps, covered, in the refrigerator for 6 weeks.

Grilled Vegetable Hash with Poached Egg and Yukon Potato

SERVES 4

This is a clean-out-the-refrigerator sort of hash that I love to serve for brunch, particularly if my friends and I had a little too much wine the night before. Seriously, this catch-all recipe is a great way to use up vegetable odds and ends in the crisper, so don't be married to the ingredients listed in the recipe; instead, let your refrigerator be your guide. For instance, post-Thanksgiving, I chop up leftover turkey and fold it into the vegetable mixture for a little added protein, or othertimes I fold in some crisp bacon. Trust me, there is no wrong way to pull this dish off successfully. Topped with a fried egg, this satisfying and healthy-ish breakfast is a winner.

4 to 6 medium Yukon Gold potatoes, scrubbed, rinsed, and dried well (about 2 pounds)

½ pound (about ½ bunch) broccolini

½ pound (about 10) button mushrooms, wiped of grit and stemmed

4 medium carrots, ends trimmed

1 large green or yellow zucchini, halved lengthwise

¼ cup extra-virgin olive oil

Fine sea salt and freshly ground black pepper

1 sweet onion, sliced into thick rounds

1 large red bell pepper

½ cup fresh flat-leaf parsley leaves, finely chopped

6 fresh thyme sprigs, leaves stripped from the stem and finely chopped

3 tablespoons grapeseed oil, plus more as needed

1 tablespoon white vinegar

8 large eggs, preferably organic and free-range

J1 Steak Sauce (page 30) or Red Wine Chipotle Barbecue Sauce (page 35), for serving (optional)

1. Preheat the oven to 425°F.

2. Prick the potatoes all over with a fork to allow steam to escape while cooking. Wrap each potato tightly with aluminum foil. Place the potatoes directly on the oven rack and bake until a fork easily pierces the potatoes without resistance, about 1 hour.

3. Rub the broccolini, mushrooms, carrots, and zucchini with 2 tablespoons of the olive oil to lightly coat. Season generously with salt. Lay the onion rounds flat on a baking sheet, drizzle with the remaining 2 tablespoons olive oil, and season with salt. You want to handle them separately so that the rings don't come apart and fall into the grill.

4. Preheat a charcoal or gas grill to medium-high heat (400 to 450°F).

5. Working in batches, place the vegetables on the grill and cook, turning periodically, until tender and lightly charred on all sides. Each vegetable takes a different amount of time,

recipe continues

anywhere from 5 to 10 minutes. Transfer the grilled vegetables to a cutting board or side platter. Place the charred bell pepper in a bowl, cover with plastic wrap, and let sweat for about 10 minutes to loosen the skin. Peel and rub off the charred skin of the bell pepper. Split the bell pepper and remove the core and seeds. Finely chop the bell pepper into small pieces. You can grill the vegetables a day ahead, if desired.

6. When the potatoes are tender, unwrap them from the foil, halve them lengthwise, and carefully scoop the flesh out into a bowl, discarding the skins. Mash the potatoes with a fork or potato masher until broken down into a chunky texture. Finely chop the grilled vegetables into ¼-inch pieces and add to the mashed potatoes, along with the roasted bell pepper, parsley, and thyme. Mix together until well combined and season with salt and pepper.

7. Heat a 10-inch cast-iron skillet or nonstick pan over medium-high heat and coat with the grapeseed oil. Add a couple of handfuls of the hash mixture. Working in batches, use a flat spatula to press the hash into an even layer, about 6 inches in diameter. Cook until golden brown on the bottom, about

5 minutes. Carefully flip the hash cake over with the spatula and brown on the other side until crispy, about 5 minutes longer. Repeat with the remaining hash mixture, adding more grapeseed oil as needed. Keep warm in a low oven or cover with a towel while you prepare the eggs.

8. To poach the eggs, fill a wide saucepan halfway with water and add the vinegar. Bring to a simmer over medium heat. When the water is just barely bubbling, carefully crack 1 egg on a flat surface—not on the lip of a bowl—into a small cup or ladle and gently pour the egg into the simmering water with one continuously slow tilt. Repeat with the remaining eggs. You can easily poach 2 or 3 eggs at a time, spacing them apart in the pot. Poach the eggs just until set but the yolks are still soft, about 2 minutes. Use a slotted spoon to transfer the eggs to a plate and dab the bottom of the eggs with paper towels to blot dry.

9. To serve, divide the hash cakes among four plates, top with 2 poached eggs, and season with salt and pepper. Drizzle with J1 Steak Sauce, if desired.

Charred Brussels Sprouts with Soft-Boiled Egg and Orange-Chili Glaze

SERVES 4 TO 6

Most people who think that they don't like these badass baby cabbages have never had them grilled crisp, tender, and served with a sweet and spicy glaze and soft drippy eggs. The complex flavor combination here hits full throttle! The key to a perfect soft-boiled egg is not to actually boil it, which makes it tough. Whether you want your egg to be runny or firm, gently cooking in barely simmering water is a must. This extraordinary side dish is welcome to join a brunch buffet or accompany the succulent Grilled Duck with Honey, Coriander, and Mint Sauce (page 100). Using a vegetable grill basket makes it easier to char the Brussels sprouts evenly and move them on and off the grill; grill baskets can be found at most kitchen or barbecue stores, as well as online.

1 cup Champagne vinegar

1 cup maple syrup

3 tablespoons unsalted butter

2 whole Calabrian chili peppers packed in oil (I like Tutto Calabria; see Note), drained, stemmed, halved lengthwise, and chopped

Finely grated zest and juice of 1 orange

1 pound Brussels sprouts, ends trimmed, tough outer leaves removed, and halved lengthwise

2 tablespoons extra-virgin olive oil, plus more for drizzling

Fine sea salt

¼ cup coarsely chopped fresh mint leaves

Juice of 1 lemon

2 to 3 large eggs, preferably organic and free-range, at room temperature

1. In a small saucepan over medium-low heat, combine the vinegar, maple syrup, butter, chili peppers, orange zest, and orange juice. Cook and stir until reduced and the glaze coats the back of a spoon, about 15 minutes. Cover and hold warm over low heat.

2. Preheat a charcoal or gas grill to medium-high heat (400 to 450°F).

3. In a medium mixing bowl, drizzle the Brussels sprouts with the 2 tablespoons olive oil and toss with your hands to coat evenly. Season with salt and toss again. Set aside.

4. Place the grill basket on the hot coals for 5 minutes to preheat. (This will help the Brussels sprouts cook more quickly and evenly.) Arrange the sprouts in an even layer in the hot grill basket and cook, turning periodically, until they are tender and charred, 6 to 8 minutes. Transfer to a serving bowl, pour in the warm glaze, add the mint and lemon juice, and season with salt. Cover and hold warm while you prepare the eggs.

Ingredient Note: Calabrian Chili Peppers
These long, red chili peppers from Calabria, Italy, add a fiery edge to any dish. Spicy, fruity, and subtly smoky at the same time, you can typically find these complex chilies jarred in oil in an Italian market or the condiment section of fine grocery stores. If not available, substitute two jarred cherry peppers or one fresh red jalapeño.

recipe continues

5. Fill a small saucepan with enough water to cover the eggs completely. Bring the water to a boil. Use a slotted spoon or strainer to gently lower the eggs into the boiling water, taking care not to drop the eggs, as they might crack. Immediately reduce the heat to very low so that the water barely bubbles. Gently boil for 6 minutes if you like your eggs with a runny yolk and tender white exterior. Boil for an additional minute if you prefer a firmer texture.

6. Use a spoon to transfer the eggs from the pot and place in a bowl of ice water. This will stop them from cooking further and cause the egg to separate somewhat from the shell, making the peeling easier. Tap the egg in various places around the larger end of the shell. Be gentle in order to leave the white intact. Hold the cracked egg under a faucet with running water and peel away the shell carefully. Reheat the peeled eggs in hot water before serving. Cut off about ¼ inch from the tops of the eggs to expose the yolks.

7. To serve, arrange the glazed Brussels sprouts on a serving platter, nestle the soft-boiled eggs cut-side up in the center of the sprouts, and drizzle olive oil over the top. Let guests dig into the oozy eggs as they like.

Singed Shishito Peppers with Sugar Snap Peas and Citrus Mango Salt

SERVES 4 TO 6

If you've never tried these little shriveled green peppers before, you're in for a real treat. Shishito peppers are the Japanese cousins to Spain's famed Padrón peppers, which may be swapped. Thankfully, shishito peppers are popping up everywhere, from farmer's markets to mainstream grocery stores like Trader Joe's and Whole Foods Market. Delicately bitter and usually mild, shishito peppers are an easy snack to throw on the grill for a pre-dinner bite. Once roasted, you'll find they take on an addictive charred-floral flavor. The refreshing crunch of sugar snap peas are the perfect foil for the smoky depth of peppers, and the Citrus Mango Salt lends a bright finish to the dish. It's easiest to use a grill basket for these little guys to prevent them from falling through the grates—if you don't have one, use a wire cooling rack.

1 pound (4 cups) shishito peppers

½ pound (2 cups) sugar snap peas, veins removed

3 tablespoons extra-virgin olive oil

½ teaspoon fine sea salt

½ cup Citrus Mango Salt (recipe follows)

1. Preheat a charcoal or gas grill to medium-high heat (400 to 450°F).

2. Combine the peppers and snap peas in a large mixing bowl and drizzle with the olive oil. Toss with your hands to coat evenly. Season with salt and toss again. Arrange the peppers and snap peas in one or two grill baskets; feel free to mix them up.

3. Put the grill baskets on the hot grill until the peppers and snap peas are tender and charred, turning often, about 5 minutes. Transfer the charred peppers and snap peas to a serving bowl and toss with 2 tablespoons of the citrus mango salt. Divide the remaining citrus mango salt into small dishes to serve on the side for guests to dip.

recipe continues

Citrus Mango Salt

MAKES ABOUT 1 CUP

Used primarily in Indian cuisine, amchoor powder (sometimes spelled amchur), is a tangy and fruity spice made from dried mango. Its tart, honey-like flavor makes a great substitute for lemon or lime juice, especially when you don't want to add moisture to a dish. Sugar and salt balance the citrus notes in this all-purpose salt—I also like to sprinkle it on fried foods for a finishing touch. Your best option for finding amchoor powder is in an Indian grocery or to order it online.

6 tablespoons amchoor powder (see Headnote)

¼ cup fine sea salt

¼ cup sugar

1 tablespoon Piment d'Espelette (see Note, page 34) or cayenne

Finely grated zest of 1 lemon

Finely grated zest of 1 orange

In a medium mixing bowl, combine the amchoor powder, salt, sugar, Piment d'Espelette, lemon zest, and orange zest. Mix well with a spoon to distribute the ingredients evenly. Transfer to a glass jar or container with a tight-fitting lid and store at room temperature (away from the heat of the stove) for up to 3 months.

Grilled Asparagus with Chopped Egg Vinaigrette

SERVES 4 TO 6

Asparagus is one of springtime's greatest gifts, when it's at the height of the season. Grilling asparagus miraculously transforms it from the vegetable you hated as a kid to something irresistible. The sweet, earthy charred flavor of the asparagus is finished with a rich egg vinaigrette that boasts the perfect amount of acidic balance. When buying asparagus, look for fat, firm stalks with deep-green or purplish tips, as they are more suited to withstand the heat of the grill and actually have better flavor than thin asparagus. Also, check the bottom of the spears—if they are dried up or moldy, chances are they have been sitting around for too long.

1 pound (2 to 3 bunches) jumbo asparagus

2 tablespoons extra-virgin olive oil

Fine sea salt

Pecorino Romano cheese to taste

½ cup Chopped Egg Vinaigrette (recipe follows)

1. Preheat a charcoal or gas grill to medium-high heat (400 to 450°F). Cut or snap off about ½ inch of the tough bottom stem of the asparagus and discard. Arrange the asparagus spears side by side on a rimmed baking sheet, drizzle with the oil, and season generously with salt. Use your hands to roll the spears around so they are evenly coated.

2. Lay the asparagus on the hot grill crosswise to the grates so they don't slip through. Cook until tender and brown in spots, rolling the spears back and forth with tongs to ensure even cooking, about 8 minutes.

3. Transfer the grilled asparagus to a serving platter. Grate the Pecorino Romano over the top, as much as you'd like, and allow to melt naturally. Spoon the egg vinaigrette across the lower-third of the asparagus. Serve the remaining vinaigrette on the side.

recipe continues

Chopped Egg Vinaigrette

MAKES 1½ CUPS

This is my take on the French classic, sauce gribiche—a hard-boiled egg sauce with punchy flavors of cornichons, vinegar, capers, and mustard. It's super versatile and also works over roasted cauliflower or potatoes, or topped on seared salmon.

2 large eggs, preferably organic and free-range, at room temperature

Finely grated zest and juice of 1 lemon

1 teaspoon fine sea salt

¼ cup grapeseed oil

¼ cup extra-virgin olive oil

1 tablespoon small (non-pareil) capers, drained

1 tablespoon finely chopped cornichons

1 tablespoon finely chopped fresh flat-leaf parsley leaves

1 tablespoon finely chopped fresh chives

1 tablespoon finely chopped fresh tarragon

1 tablespoon finely chopped fresh chervil

¼ teaspoon Piment d'Espelette (see Note, page 34) or cayenne

1. Take the eggs out of the refrigerator about 30 minutes before you plan to boil them; this will prevent them from cracking in the water. Bring a saucepan of water to a boil over medium-high heat. Gently lower the eggs into the boiling water with a spoon. Reduce to medium heat and gently boil the eggs for 10 minutes.

2. In the meantime, prepare an ice bath by filling a large bowl halfway with water and adding a tray of ice cubes. The key here is to cool the eggs quickly. Why? It's the best way to prevent discoloration around the yolk and makes them easier to peel.

3. Using a strainer or slotted spoon, transfer the eggs to the ice bath. Allow them to sit in the water for 5 minutes until they are completely cooled down to the center.

4. Take an egg and give it a few gentle taps on the kitchen counter; you want to crack the shell while trying not to damage the white underneath. Gently roll the egg around until the shell has small cracks all over it and peel it off. Repeat with the remaining egg.

5. Using a paring knife, halve the eggs lengthwise and pop the yolks out into a mixing bowl— reserve the egg whites. Smash the yolks with the back of a fork. Add 2 tablespoons water, lemon juice (reserve the zest for adding with the herbs), and salt, mashing with the fork to make a paste. Slowly drizzle in the grapeseed oil and olive oil in a slow, steady stream while gently blending with a small whisk or fork until the egg mixture is smooth and thick and looks like mayonnaise. Add the capers, cornichons, parsley, chives, tarragon, chervil, lemon zest, and Piment d'Espelette. Coarsely chop the egg whites, add them to the bowl, and gently fold them in until well coated in the yolk mixture. The vinaigrette may be made up to 2 days in advance and stored, covered, in the refrigerator.

Blistered Broccolini with Rosemary and Lemon Bread Crumbs

SERVES 4 TO 6

New to broccolini? It looks and tastes a lot like broccoli, but it's just a hint sweeter and has long, tender stalks with smaller florets at the top. Grilling really concentrates the natural sugars and gives the broccolini an especially nutty flavor. This straightforward dish is one you'll find yourself making over and over again.

1½ pounds (3 to 4 bunches) broccolini

4 garlic cloves, minced after removing the germ (see Note, page 31)

3 tablespoons extra-virgin olive oil

½ teaspoon fine sea salt

2 tablespoons Asian chili oil

Juice of 1 lemon

¼ cup Lemon Bread Crumbs (recipe follows)

2 tablespoons fresh rosemary leaves, coarsely chopped

1. Preheat a charcoal or gas grill to medium-high heat (400 to 450°F).

2. Combine the broccolini and garlic in a large mixing bowl and drizzle with the olive oil, tossing with your hands to coat evenly. Season with the salt and toss again. Lay the broccolini across the grill grates and cook until tender and charred, turning often, 8 to 10 minutes. Transfer the broccolini to a serving platter. Drizzle with the chili oil and lemon juice. Evenly sprinkle the bread crumbs and rosemary over the top.

Lemon Bread Crumbs

MAKES 2 CUPS

This is one of my essential kitchen staples to add texture to pasta, sprinkle on vegetables, or dust over seafood (see Grilled Calamari with Blue Lake Green Beans, Almonds, and Lemon Bread Crumbs, page 89). For people who are maintaining a gluten-free diet and can't eat bread crumbs, I swap store-bought puffed quinoa in its place, which is delicious in its own right. See the variation.

2 cups panko bread crumbs

¼ cup grated Parmesan cheese

½ teaspoon fine sea salt

¼ teaspoon freshly ground black pepper

8 tablespoons (1 stick) unsalted butter

Finely grated zest of 2 lemons

1. In a small mixing bowl, combine the bread crumbs, Parmesan, salt, and pepper with a rubber spatula. Set aside.

2. Heat a 10-inch sauté pan over low heat and add the butter. Allow the butter to melt slowly; do not let it bubble. Add the bread crumb mixture to the pan and raise to medium-high heat. Cook, stirring constantly with the spatula, until the bread crumbs are toasted and dark golden brown. Sprinkle in the lemon zest and mix well to incorporate. Remove from the heat and transfer to a rimmed baking sheet to cool. Store in an airtight container at room temperature for up to 1 week.

GLUTEN-FREE VARIATION

You can make a gluten-free variation of this recipe with store-bought puffed quinoa. Simply replace the panko with the quinoa and mix it with the Parmesan, salt, pepper, and zest—no need to fry it in butter since the quinoa is already "puffed." Store in an airtight container at room temperature for up to 1 week.

Grilled Summer Squash
with Charred Tomato Sauce and Parmesan

SERVES 4 TO 6

Living in Los Angeles, we are so fortunate to have the bounty of produce at the Santa Monica Farmers Market twice a week. It's just a few blocks away from one of my other restaurants, Mélisse, and in the summertime it's well stocked with a huge variety of squash and tomatoes. There are many different varieties of summer squash, each with a distinct shape, color, and flavor. Take advantage of what your farmer's market or grocer has to offer and buy an assortment of squash to shine in this dish.

2 medium yellow squash, halved lengthwise and then crosswise

2 medium zucchini, halved lengthwise and then crosswise

4 pattypan or starburst squash, halved through the stem

½ pound whole baby summer squash, such as zephyr, halved lengthwise

¼ cup extra-virgin olive oil

½ teaspoon fine sea salt

1 cup Charred Tomato Sauce, at room temperature (recipe follows)

4 ounces Parmesan cheese

Fleur de sel

Freshly ground black pepper

1. Combine the varieties of squash in a large mixing bowl and drizzle with the olive oil; season with salt. Preheat a charcoal or gas grill to medium-high heat (400 to 450°F). Lay the squash on the hot grill, cut-sides down, and cook until tender and slightly charred, turning periodically with tongs to prevent burning. Take care not to overcook; the squash should be tender but still firm. Transfer the grilled squash to a side platter as they become done.

2. Spoon the charred tomato sauce evenly on a serving platter. Arrange the grilled squash on the sauce and grate the Parmesan over the top, as much as you'd like, and allow to melt naturally. Sprinkle the squash with a few flakes of fleur de sel and finish with 3 turns of a peppermill.

recipe continues

Charred Tomato Sauce

MAKES 2 CUPS

Raw, grilled, or roasted, tomatoes are my favorite summer bounty. Charring tomatoes on the grill amplifies their natural sugars and gives this simple summer sauce its backbone. Castelvetrano are bright green olives from Sicily that are gaining popularity for their irresistibly smooth, buttery flavor and firm texture. Supported by the salty finish of anchovy and the floral brightness of the fresh herbs, this robust tomato sauce wakes up the flavor of subtle vegetables, like zucchini, and makes the perfect light summer supper tossed with hot spaghetti.

2 large heirloom or beefsteak tomatoes

½ cup extra-virgin olive oil, plus more for rubbing the tomatoes

¼ cup fresh flat-leaf parsley leaves, coarsely chopped

¼ cup fresh basil leaves, coarsely chopped

3 fresh thyme sprigs, leaves stripped from the stems and coarsely chopped

6 marinated white anchovy fillets (boquerones), drained and chopped

6 Castelvetrano olives, flesh cut off close to the pits and chopped

3 tablespoons red wine vinegar

2 garlic cloves, grated after removing the germ (see Note, page 31)

½ teaspoon fine sea salt

½ teaspoon dried red pepper flakes

1. Preheat a charcoal or gas grill to high heat (500°F).

2. Rub the tomato skins well with olive oil to prevent them from sticking to the grill. Put the tomatoes on the grill and cook until shriveled and charred on all sides, turning periodically, about 10 minutes. Transfer the tomatoes to a side platter to cool slightly. Peel off the skins and cut out the cores of the tomatoes and discard. Put the tomato flesh into a fine-mesh strainer set over a bowl to drain out some of the tomato water, reserving the tomato water; this should take about 5 minutes. Transfer the strained tomatoes to a small mixing bowl and mash with a fork or potato masher until broken down into a chunky texture.

3. Add the remaining ½ cup olive oil, the parsley, basil, thyme, anchovies, olives, vinegar, garlic, salt, and red pepper flakes. Toss to distribute the ingredients evenly. Add some of the tomato water back in if the sauce consistency looks too thick. The sauce may be stored, covered, in the refrigerator for up to 1 week.

Grilled Stuffed Portobello Mushrooms with Escarole

SERVES 4

This simple vegetarian dish is earthy, easy, and satisfying. The big, meaty texture of the mushrooms stands up beautifully to the grill heat. Fluffy couscous makes a satisfying stuffing for the mushrooms because it's so moist and keeps the mushrooms from drying out on the grill. Cooking the escarole mellows out its bitter flavor and adds subtle smokiness. The currants and nuts in the stuffing lend sweetness and crunch, and the flavorful lemon vinaigrette is soaked up into everything. Win! This dish is deliciously quick and comes together in about 15 minutes. Serve as an appetizer, side dish, or light vegetarian meal.

5 large portobello mushroom caps, wiped of grit

Extra-virgin olive oil

Fine sea salt

1 head escarole, rinsed, dried, and halved through the core

½ cup dry couscous

¼ cup currants

¼ cup fresh mint leaves, chopped

2 tablespoons pine nuts, toasted

Lemon Vinaigrette (page 91)

Freshly ground black pepper

Fleur de sel

1. Preheat a charcoal or gas grill to medium heat (350°F).

2. Lay the mushrooms flat on a rimmed baking sheet, drizzle generously with olive oil, and season with salt. Place all of the mushrooms on the grill, gill-side down, and cook for 5 minutes. Remove 4 of the mushrooms to a side plate; these will be stuffed. Flip the remaining mushroom over and grill the cap side for 5 minutes. Transfer the mushroom to a cutting board and finely chop.

3. Season the escarole lightly with salt and place cut-side on the grill. Grill until it is nicely charred, 3 to 4 minutes. Turn the escarole over with tongs and grill the other side for 2 to 3 minutes. Transfer the escarole to a cutting board, cut out the core, and coarsely chop; you want to keep a bit of texture.

4. Combine ½ cup water and ¼ teaspoon salt in a small pot and bring to a boil over high heat. Stir in the couscous and remove from the heat; cover with a lid and allow the couscous to absorb the water, about 5 minutes. Fluff the couscous with a fork to gently break apart the grains. Transfer the couscous to a medium mixing bowl and add the chopped mushrooms, escarole, currants, mint, and pine nuts. Drizzle with the vinaigrette, season with salt and 3 or 4 turns of a peppermill, and toss to combine.

5. Spoon the couscous mixture into the mushroom caps to fill and patting down lightly. Put the stuffed mushrooms on the grill, stuffing-side up. Close the lid and open the vent to maintain medium heat. Cook for 5 minutes, until the bottoms of the mushrooms are charred. Sprinkle with a little fleur de sel and serve warm.

Grilled Orata with Herb Yogurt

SERVES 4

Orata (also called sea bream and dorade) is a mouthwatering fish hailing from the coastal waters of the Mediterranean. While tender, this delicately fleshed fish doesn't fall apart on the grill and stays moist, and the skin crisps up beautifully. Brushing with the herb yogurt sauce not only imparts fabulous flavor but the fat in the yogurt and mayonnaise helps protect the fish from drying out and sticking to the grill. Save yourself the hassle and have your fish guy fillet the orata for you; that's what they're there for. If sea bream is not available, substitute another thin fillet fish, like red snapper. Serve with Grilled Asparagus with Chopped Egg Vinaigrette (page 73).

¾ cup plain whole-milk Greek yogurt

¼ cup mayonnaise

Juice of ½ lemon

1 teaspoon fine sea salt, plus more for seasoning

Pinch of cayenne

1 bunch fresh flat-leaf parsley leaves, coarsely chopped

1 bunch fresh mint leaves, coarsely chopped

½ bunch fresh cilantro leaves, coarsely chopped

Vegetable oil, for greasing the grill

Two 1½- to 2-pound skin-on sea bream fish (orata), scaled, filleted, and pin bones removed

2 lemons, halved crosswise, for serving

1. In a high-speed blender, such as a Vitamix, combine the yogurt, mayonnaise, lemon juice, salt, cayenne, parsley, mint, and cilantro. Puree until the mixture is completely smooth and bright green, about 4 minutes, and then transfer to a container and set aside. The yogurt sauce can be easily made the day before you plan on serving. If prepared ahead of time, keep it covered and refrigerated.

2. Preheat a charcoal or gas grill to high heat (500°F).

3. Take a few paper towels and fold them several times to make a thick square. Blot a small amount of vegetable oil on the paper towel, then carefully and quickly wipe the hot grates of the grill. This will create a nonstick grilling surface.

4. Brush the fish with the yogurt sauce on both sides. Season lightly with salt. Lay the fish fillets on the hot grill, skin-side down and sear for 3 to 5 minutes. Turn the fish over and grill the flesh side for 2 minutes.

5. While cooking the fish, place the lemons on the grill, flesh-side down. Cook until the lemon juice starts to ooze and the flesh is nicely charred, about 4 minutes. Arrange the fish fillets on a warm serving platter, skin-side up. Serve with the grilled lemons and remaining yogurt sauce on the side.

Seared Scallops with Carrot Juice, Tamarind, and Rosemary

SERVES 4 TO 6

Scallops are one of my all-time favorite foods—they are elegant, easy, and tailor-made for the grill. After a short stint over the fire, they come out succulent, silky, and sweet. Start by assessing the scallops at the fish market. I usually inspect every one just to make sure they're all in perfect shape, i.e., not torn, and fresh with a sweet ocean smell. If you're not convinced the scallops are at their peak, use shrimp for this recipe instead. To ensure scallop success, it's important that your grill is impeccably clean without any black residue on the grates; this not only helps to avoid sticking but also prevents any black flecks from tainting the look of the milky-white flesh. Scallops are delicate; brushing them with mayonnaise adds another layer of protection so they don't stick to the grill and flare up like an oil can. The brightly colored and tangy carrot sauce pairs perfectly with the subtle sweetness of the scallops; together, this dish exemplifies the balance of texture, flavor, and visual appeal.

1 cup fresh carrot juice

¼ cup honey

¼ cup freshly squeezed lemon juice

Juice of ½ lime

3 tablespoons tamarind paste

1 teaspoon fine sea salt, plus more to taste

1 large fresh rosemary sprig, leaves stripped from the stem

½ cup grapeseed oil

12 large sea scallops (about 1 pound), muscle removed

¼ cup mayonnaise

¼ cup nasturtium leaves and flowers (optional)

1. Combine the carrot juice, honey, lemon juice, lime juice, tamarind paste, and salt in a small saucepan and place over medium-high heat. Bring to a boil for 30 seconds to dissolve the honey and tamarind. Stir in the rosemary; remove from the heat and cover. Let stand for 10 minutes to infuse the rosemary flavor into the sauce. Pour the sauce through a fine-mesh strainer into a blender. Blend on low speed until smooth. While the motor is running, pour in the grapeseed oil in a slow, steady stream until emulsified.

2. Lay the scallops side by side on several layers of paper towels to drain any excess natural liquid; make sure both sides are completely dry, as wet scallops do not cook well. Brush both sides of the scallops lightly with the mayonnaise and sprinkle with salt—the mayonnaise prevents the scallops from sticking to the grill and helps the salt stick.

3. Preheat a charcoal or gas grill to high heat (500°F).

4. Place the scallops on the hot grill for 2 minutes, carefully turn them over, and grill the other side until they have a nice char, about 1 minute. Scallops are a little delicate; if one seems to stick, don't try to pull it up, or you risk tearing it. Give it another 30 seconds and then try again.

5. To serve, drizzle the carrot sauce on a serving platter and arrange the scallops on top. Garnish with nasturtium leaves and flowers, if using.

Oysters with Shallots and Basque Vinegar

SERVES 4 TO 6

Raw oysters are great. Seriously, I love them. But sometimes throwing them on the grill is so much better. The flame concentrates that briny flavor while gently poaching the oysters inside. Plus, the heat naturally pops the shells open, so there's no shucking necessary. Large oysters hold up to the heat of the grill better than smaller varieties. When buying oysters, look for ones that are closed and without any cracked shells. The vinegar sauce is my take on classic mignonette, and then I top the oysters with a bit of lemony bread crumbs à la Rockefeller. Serve as a starter.

¼ cup Basque Vinegar (page 34)

1 shallot, finely chopped

2 tablespoons finely chopped fresh chives

2 teaspoons coarsely cracked black pepper

18 large oysters, such as Hama Hama, Fanny Bay, or Beausoleil, scrubbed clean

Rock salt, for serving

1 teaspoon fleur de sel

¼ cup Lemon Bread Crumbs (page 77)

1. In a small mixing bowl, combine the vinegar, shallot, chives, and pepper. Set aside at room temperature.

2. Preheat a charcoal or gas grill to high heat (500°F).

3. Place the oysters cupped-side down on the grill grate. Cover the grill and cook until the oysters open, about 2 minutes. Using tongs, transfer the oysters to a platter (discard any that do not open). Using an oyster knife, remove the top shells and loosen the oysters from the bottom. Cut the muscle away from the top shell, then bend the shell back and discard it. Run the knife underneath the oyster to detach it completely but leave it in the shell. Be careful not to spill its delicious juice.

4. Arrange the oysters on a large platter covered with rock salt to steady them. Sprinkle each with a few flakes of fleur de sel. Spoon about 1 tablespoon of the vinegar mixture on top of each oyster and finish with about 1 teaspoon of the toasted bread crumbs.

Grilled Calamari with Blue Lake Green Beans, Almonds, and Lemon Bread Crumbs

SERVES 4 TO 6

Calamari has a natural chewy quality and delicate flavor that I find benefits from salting before grilling to extract moisture and cure a little bit first. When grilling calamari, timing is key; if it sits too long after it's cooked, it becomes rubbery and dry. So when you prepare this dish at home, get all the components together first and grill the calamari last to maintain its melt-in-your-mouth texture. Any green beans will work for this summer dish, but I prefer Blue Lakes for their crispness and ability to stand up to the vibrant lemon vinaigrette. The bean's unique flavor is distinctively mild, subtly grassy, and sweet, with a crisp-tender texture. This dish makes an impressive appetizer or light main meal. Enjoy with a chilled glass of dry white wine or rosé.

½ pound (18 pieces) calamari tubes, cleaned, rinsed, and patted dry

Fine sea salt

½ pound green beans, preferably Blue Lake, ends trimmed

Vegetable oil, for greasing the grill

Extra-virgin olive oil, for coating

1 cup cherry tomatoes, halved lengthwise

½ cup fresh flat-leaf parsley leaves, finely chopped

¼ cup sliced almonds, toasted

2 tablespoons finely chopped fresh chives

1 small shallot, minced

¼ teaspoon Piment d'Espelette (see Note, page 34) or cayenne

¼ cup Lemon Vinaigrette (recipe follows)

Juice of ½ lemon

¼ cup Lemon Bread Crumbs (page 77)

1. Set a wire rack insert inside a rimmed baking sheet. Lay the calamari side by side on the rack and season generously with salt. Flip the calamari over and season the other side with salt. Set aside at room temperature for 30 minutes—this process of salting and sitting extracts some of the excess seawater from the calamari, so they grill up nice and firm. Rinse the calamari well and pat dry inside and out with paper towels. Remove the wire rack from the baking sheet and wipe out the excess seawater drained from the calamari. Line several layers of paper towels on the baking sheet and line up the calamari side by side. Cover with several layers of paper towels to prevent the calamari from drying out and set aside in the refrigerator for up to 8 hours in advance.

2. Bring a large pot of well-salted water to a boil over high heat. Prepare an ice bath by filling a large bowl halfway with water and adding a tray of ice cubes. Set a colander or mesh strainer inside the ice water.

recipe continues

3. Blanch the green beans until tender when pierced with a knife, about 2 minutes.

4. Use a slotted spoon to transfer the green beans from the boiling water and plunge them into the ice bath to "shock" them, which will stop the cooking process and cool them down right away. This will also lock in the bright green color. Once completely cool, pull out the colander or strainer to drain the beans. Pat them dry with paper towels, cut them into thirds, and set aside. The green beans can be easily prepared in advance, covered, and refrigerated.

5. Preheat a charcoal or gas grill to very high heat (650 to 700°F).

6. Take a few paper towels and fold them several times to make a thick square. Blot a small amount of vegetable oil on the paper towel, then carefully and quickly wipe the hot grates of the grill. This will create a nonstick grilling surface. Lightly coat the calamari with olive oil. Put the blanched green beans in a grill basket and place on the hot grill. Lay the calamari across the grates and grill each side for 2½ minutes, turning carefully with tongs.

7. Transfer the grilled green beans to a large mixing bowl. Cut the calamari into ½-inch rings and add to the bowl. Add the tomatoes, parsley, almonds, chives, shallot, ½ teaspoon salt, and the Piment d'Espelette. Toss well to combine thoroughly. Pour in the vinaigrette and lemon juice and toss well until coated evenly. Transfer to a large serving bowl. Sprinkle evenly with the bread crumbs just before serving.

Lemon Vinaigrette

MAKES ½ CUP

This classic vinaigrette is a go-to multipurpose dressing, and thankfully this recipe can easily be doubled so it's always on hand. Be sure to try it on a simple butter lettuce salad or over any of your favorite grilled vegetables. Grapeseed oil has a clean, light taste that balances out the fruitiness of olive oil.

Juice of 1 lemon

2 teaspoons caster (superfine) sugar

1 teaspoon fine sea salt

¼ cup grapeseed oil

¼ cup extra-virgin olive oil

In a jar or container with a tight-fitting lid, combine the lemon juice, sugar, and salt. Secure the lid and shake well. Add the grapeseed oil and olive oil and shake well again. The vinaigrette may be stored covered in the refrigerator for up to 3 months. Shake to re-emulsify before using.

Chicken Skewers with Backyard Tomato Glaze

SERVES 4 TO 6

I've been making this tomato glaze since I was in my twenties and it never disappoints. This dish is the most tender and most flavorful chicken you will ever make! The chicken is marinated in a tomato, honey, cilantro, and soy sauce bath for a few hours, skewered, and then grilled. It's best to skewer the dark and white meat separately to ensure consistent cooking times. Super easy and always a hit, this is a veritable crowd-pleaser. The chicken marinates for several hours, so plan accordingly. Serve with Little Gems with Flavors of Caesar (page 225) or your favorite fresh green salad.

Special Equipment

24 wooden skewers, soaked in water for 1 to 2 hours to prevent them from burning on the grill

2½ pounds skinless, boneless chicken thighs, cut into 1-inch chunks

2½ pounds skinless, boneless chicken breasts, cut into 1-inch chunks

Backyard Tomato Glaze (recipe follows)

Vegetable oil, for greasing the grill

2 tablespoons extra-virgin olive oil

Fine sea salt

1. Thread five pieces of the chicken thighs onto twelve of the skewers, leaving a little gap in between the chunks to allow the glaze to get in between. Do the same for the chicken breasts with the remaining twelve skewers, folding the pieces in half if they are long and thin. Lay the skewers side by side on a rimmed baking sheet and pour the glaze over the chicken to coat all sides, rolling the skewers over so they are fully covered. Cover with plastic wrap and refrigerate for 6 hours or up to overnight to marinate. Take the chicken out of the refrigerator about 30 minutes before grilling so it can come up to room temperature.

2. Be sure the charcoal or gas grill is clean, and then preheat to medium heat (350°F).

3. To grease the grill, lightly dip a wad of paper towels in vegetable oil and, using tongs, carefully rub over the grates several times until glossy and coated. Drizzle the chicken skewers with the olive oil and season well with salt.

4. Place the thighs on the grill first because they take longer to cook, and grill for 4 to 6 minutes, turning periodically so each side gets a nice char. After the thighs get a head start, put the chicken breast skewers on the

recipe continues

CHARCOAL

grill, turning periodically, until the white meat is tender and slightly charred and the glaze is sticky, 6 to 8 minutes. Continue to grill the thigh skewers for a total of 10 to 12 minutes. Transfer the chicken skewers from the grill to a serving platter as they become done. Alternatively, you can serve the skewers in rocks glasses, wood-handle side up, so guests can easily grab them. Drizzle any remaining glaze over the top or serve it alongside.

Backyard Tomato Glaze

MAKES ABOUT 3 CUPS

This spicy, sticky glaze is a winner for just about any chicken dish, and you can also enjoy it on chicken you roast in the oven. The acidic, fruity tomato, combined with the floral flavor of lemongrass and cilantro, the liveliness of ginger, and salty-umami of soy adds a compelling brightness to the meat. You can easily double the glaze recipe if you want to serve extra on the side with the chicken skewers.

2 tablespoons grapeseed oil

1 sweet onion, sliced

2 lemongrass stalks, tough outer layers removed, smashed, and chopped into 2-inch pieces

3 garlic cloves, smashed after removing the germ (see Note, page 31)

One 1-inch piece fresh ginger, peeled and sliced into ¼-inch pieces

½ jalapeño, seeded if desired

1¼ cups honey

1¼ cups soy sauce

¾ cup unseasoned rice wine vinegar

1 quart low-sodium tomato juice

15 fresh cilantro sprigs

2 tablespoons chopped fresh cilantro

Juice of 1 lemon

1. Coat a medium saucepan with the grapeseed oil and place over medium heat. Add the onion, lemongrass, garlic, ginger, and jalapeño. Cook and stir until the vegetables begin to soften and smell fragrant, about 5 minutes. Stir in the honey and simmer until it begins to bubble and turn a dark amber color, 5 to 6 minutes. Pour in the soy sauce and vinegar and gently simmer until reduced by half, about 5 minutes. Pour in the tomato juice and add the cilantro sprigs, raise to medium-high heat, and bring to a boil.

2. Reduce to medium-low heat and simmer, skimming off any foam that rises to the surface, until the sauce is thick, dark red, and coats the back of a spoon, 40 to 45 minutes. Pour the glaze through a fine-mesh strainer into a medium heatproof bowl, pushing the solids with the back of a wooden spoon. Discard the solids. Once cooled, add the chopped cilantro and lemon juice.

Chicken Salsa Verde

SERVES 4

Whole grilled chicken is a thing of beauty. The hardest part of this recipe is boning the chicken, so I suggest asking your butcher to do it for you to save time and effort. Do check carefully that there are no bones or cartilage left behind. Boning the entire chicken allows it to lie flat on the grill, and in turn it cooks more quickly and evenly. The chimichurri is oil- and vinegar-based, so I avoid getting it on the chicken skin when marinating it, as the extra oil can cause flare-ups and the acidic vinegar tends to make the skin rubbery. This dish is a mainstay when grilling for my family and friends on the weekend in my backyard. Serve with your favorite sides or the Collard Greens with Yam, Shaved Onion, Aged Cheddar, and Raisin-Caper Vinaigrette (page 227).

2 cups Smoked Paprika Chimichurri with Pickled Mustard Seeds (page 33)

¼ cup sherry vinegar or Basque Vinegar (page 34)

One 3- to 4-pound whole chicken, wings removed, halved, and boned

Vegetable oil, for greasing the grill

Extra-virgin olive oil, for drizzling

Fleur de sel

1. In a small mixing bowl, combine the chimichurri with the vinegar. Reserve 1 cup for serving.

2. Pour the remaining 1¼ cups of the sauce on a rimmed baking sheet and spread in an even layer. Lay the chicken in the marinade, flesh-side down, being sure to coat the sauce in every part of the meat but not on the skin. You want to take care not to get the oil-based marinade on the chicken skin as it will cause flare-ups and burn more quickly on the grill; it will not allow the fat to render or the skin to crisp up nicely. Marinate the chicken uncovered in the refrigerator for at least 6 hours or preferably overnight. Take the chicken out of the refrigerator about 30 minutes before cooking to allow the chicken to come up to room temperature.

3. Preheat a charcoal or gas grill to medium heat (300 to 350°F).

4. Take a few paper towels and fold them several times to make a thick square. Blot a small amount of vegetable oil on the paper towel, then carefully and quickly wipe the hot grates of the grill. This will create a nonstick grilling surface.

5. Season both sides of the chicken generously with salt. Carefully lay the chicken skin-side down on the grill. Close the lid and open the vent slightly to maintain a medium heat (around 300 to 350°F). You'll need to open and close the vents or lid to maintain the temperature. Slowly cook until all the fat is rendered, 30 to 35 minutes, opening the lid and moving the chicken if necessary to prevent flare-ups. Turn the chicken over and grill the flesh side, uncovered, until no longer pink, 4 to 5 minutes. An instant-read thermometer inserted into the thickest part of the breast should read 162°F.

6. Transfer the chicken skin-side up to a wire rack and rest for about 5 minutes to allow the juices to recirculate. Slice the chicken and arrange on a serving platter. Drizzle the chicken with olive oil and finish with a sprinkle of fleur de sel. Serve with the remaining sauce on the side.

Mom's Honey Chicken

SERVES 4

My mother, Huli, was a big influence and inspiration on my becoming a chef. She was a well-known caterer back in the day and owned a prominent cooking school in Santa Monica, where I grew up. After cooking professionally all day, she would then come home and prepare dinner for my two sisters and me. Her baked honey chicken was the one meal our entire family could unanimously agree upon. Using accessible ingredients like soy sauce, honey, lemon, and mustard, this dish is a simple, craveable crowd-pleaser and deserves a spot on your permanent roster. I updated my mom's recipe by grilling the chicken, as it adds another layer of smoky flavor to an already terrific dish. Serve with your favorite sides, such as Blistered Broccolini with Rosemary and Lemon Bread Crumbs (page 76). Thanks, Mom!

¾ cup soy sauce

½ cup honey

1 tablespoon sesame oil

2 garlic cloves, crushed after removing the germ (see Note, page 31)

One 1-inch piece fresh ginger, peeled and grated (about 1 tablespoon)

1 tablespoon Dijon mustard

1 tablespoon fresh thyme leaves

Finely grated zest of 1 lemon

8 boneless, skin-on chicken thighs (about 2 pounds)

1 teaspoon fine sea salt

1 tablespoon Lemon Pepper (page 45), plus more for serving

Vegetable oil, for greasing the grill

6 scallions (green parts only), chopped, for serving

¼ cup fresh mint leaves, chopped, for serving

1. In a small mixing bowl, combine the soy, honey, sesame oil, garlic, ginger, mustard, thyme, and lemon zest with a whisk. Pour the marinade into a baking dish and spread it out evenly. Arrange the chicken thighs flesh-side down in the marinade so that the marinade covers the flesh only and just reaches the skin. You want to take care not to get the marinade on the chicken skin as it will cause it to caramelize and burn more quickly on the grill and not allow the fat to render or the skin to crisp up. Marinate the chicken uncovered in the refrigerator for 3½ to 4 hours. Take the chicken out of the refrigerator about 30 minutes before cooking so that it comes up to room temperature.

2. Preheat a charcoal or gas grill to medium heat (350°F).

3. Take a few paper towels and fold them several times to make a thick square. Blot a small amount of vegetable oil on the paper towel, then carefully and quickly wipe the hot grates of the grill. This will create a nonstick grilling surface.

4. Season the chicken with the salt and lemon pepper. Cook until all the fat is rendered out, 30 to 35 minutes. This will create crispy, golden skin. Move the chicken as necessary to prevent sticking. Turn the chicken over and grill the flesh side, uncovered, until no longer pink, 3 to 4 minutes. An instant-read thermometer inserted into the thickest part of the chicken should read 170°F.

5. Transfer the chicken skin-side up to a wire rack and let rest for about 5 minutes to allow the juices to recirculate. Arrange the chicken on a serving platter. Season with additional lemon pepper and scatter the scallions and mint over top.

Grilled Duck with Honey, Coriander, and Mint Sauce

SERVES 4

Fancier than chicken and more elegant than turkey, duck is a delectable departure from the usual dinner. The most important step in grilling duck is that you need to remove the copious amounts of fat in the skin. At Charcoal, we hang our ducks for 3 weeks in a temperature-controlled aging fridge adjacent to the dining room before we butcher and grill. The dry-aging process helps melt the fat away and prevents the grease from causing flare-ups, which can burn the duck. You can achieve a similar result at home by pricking the skin and drying the duck on a wire rack in the refrigerator for several days so that air circulates all around. Butterflying the duck makes it easier to cook and shortens the grilling time, and the result is thin, crispy skin with succulent meat.

The honey, coriander, and mint glaze brings out a fresh, herbal brightness to the richness of the duck.

One (5-pound) whole Pekin or Long Island duck, neck and giblets removed

¾ cup honey

15 fresh mint leaves, finely chopped

1½ tablespoons toasted coriander seeds, coarsely ground

2 teaspoons coarsely cracked black pepper

½ teaspoon fine sea salt, plus more for seasoning

Fleur de sel

Freshly ground black pepper

Extra-virgin olive oil

½ bunch fresh mint sprigs, coarsely chopped, for serving

1. Dry the duck skin with paper towels to remove excess moisture. Lay the duck on a rimmed baking sheet fitted with a wire rack. Prick the duck skin, not the flesh, at a slight angle all over with a sharp knife or metal skewer—this will help render the fat. Put in the refrigerator, uncovered, for at least 48 hours and up to 5 days to allow to air-dry. This process with help the skin become crispier during the grilling.

2. Using a boning knife, cut off all the neck fat and save it for another use. (You can render the fat in a skillet over low heat and pour off the liquid gold, refrigerate, and use for frying potatoes, eggs, or greens.) Remove the wishbone from the inside of the neck area. Working top to bottom, cut lengthwise straight down along either side of the breast bone to release one of the breasts from the carcass. Make long incisions, working the tip of the knife all of the way down to the breast plate. Use your hand to pull the breast away from the body and continue to cut, following along the leg and thigh at the bottom and the wing at

recipe continues

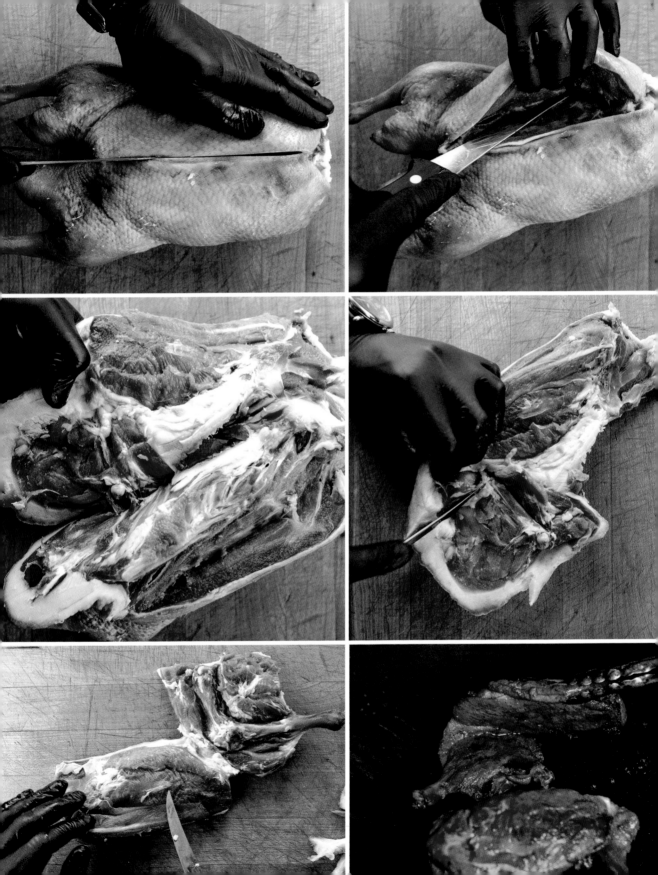

the top. You should now have a breast of duck with the leg and thigh attached, and the wing left on the carcass. Flip the detached breast and leg skin-side down on your cutting board and cut along the L-shaped leg bone to expose the meat, but do not remove the bone. Use your fingers to pull the leg meat away from the bone so it lies flat—this is key to even cooking. Now, go back in and repeat on the other side of the duck, using the breast bone as your guide and keeping the breast attached to the leg and thigh.

3. Heat the honey in a small saucepan over medium-low heat until it begins to bubble and turn a dark amber color, about 5 minutes. Add the mint, coriander, 1 tablespoon water, the cracked pepper, and the salt. Mix until well combined. Simmer and stir to infuse the flavors into the honey, 1 to 2 minutes. Do not reduce. Remove from the heat and reserve at room temperature.

4. Preheat a charcoal or gas grill to medium-high heat (400°F).

5. Season both the skin and flesh side of the two duck halves generously with salt and place skin-side down on the grill grate. Close the lid and open the grill vents just slightly to maintain a medium heat of around 400°F. This will allow the duck skin to slowly render while the flesh cooks gently. As the duck is continuing

to cook, monitor the heat and watch out for flare-ups. After about 12 minutes, the duck skin will become golden brown and crisp, the breast will be nearly cooked to medium-rare, but you'll need to cook the leg and thigh a bit longer. Open the lid and flip the duck over so it is now skin-side up, and fold the breast on top of the leg and thigh so it is not directly on the grill. Continue to cook for 5 minutes—this allows the dark leg meat to cook thoroughly while keeping the breast off the heat to protect it from overcooking.

6. Flip the breast back down so all of the skin is now faceup. Once the leg is completely cooked, brush the skin of the entire duck with a light coating of the honey-coriander glaze. Flip the duck back over to skin-side down to allow the honey to caramelize on the surface of the skin. Brush the meat side of the duck, too, and cook for 1 minute. Remove the duck from the heat and allow it to rest on a wire rack for 10 minutes before slicing and serving.

7. To serve: Separate the breasts from the leg portions. Carve the breasts crosswise and cut each duck leg into two pieces. Arrange the legs and thighs in the center of a serving platter and fan the sliced duck breasts around in a circle. Drizzle the remaining glaze over and around the duck. Season with fleur de sel, 6 turns of a peppermill, and a drizzle of olive oil. Scatter the mint over the top.

J1-Marinated Skirt Steak

SERVES 4

In my opinion, skirt steak is really only good when cooked on a grill. The thin, long cut of beef is lean in fat yet rich in flavor and loves the intensity of high heat. Not to be confused with tougher flank steak (though it may be substituted), skirt steak is one of the only meats I find benefits from marinating because marinating not only helps tenderize the meat but also intensifies its distinctive beefiness. My signature J1 Steak Sauce (page 30) makes a bold steak marinade that really packs in the flavor, and the sugar in it lends a nice char to the meat. This grilled skirt steak is an easy, quick meal for any night of the week and goes with virtually anything in this book, from the Grilled Chopped Vegetable Salad with Havarti, Bacon, Kalamata Olives, and Jo-Jo's Vinaigrette (page 61) to Roasted Radishes with Butter and Sea Salt (page 131).

Due to its length, skirt steak is usually sold folded or rolled up. Because it's so long, the meat tends to hang off the grill, so I cut it in half down the middle into shorter pieces so it fits nicely.

CHARCOAL

2 pounds skirt steak, halved crosswise

1½ cups J1 Steak Sauce (page 30)

Vegetable oil, for greasing the grill

2 teaspoons fine sea salt

Fleur de sel

Freshly ground black pepper

1. Lay the skirt steak flat in a large baking dish and pour 1 cup of the J1 Steak Sauce evenly on top. Spread the sauce out to cover the surface, and then turn the meat over to coat both sides evenly. Set aside in the refrigerator to marinate for at least 2 hours or up to overnight, so the flavors can sink in a bit. Take the meat out of the refrigerator about 30 minutes before grilling so that it comes up to room temperature.

2. Preheat a charcoal or gas grill to high heat (500°F).

3. Take a few paper towels and fold them several times to make a thick square. Blot a small amount of vegetable oil on the paper towel, then carefully and quickly wipe the hot grates of the grill. This will create a nonstick grilling surface.

4. Season the meat on both sides lightly with the sea salt. Lay the steak on the grill and cook, turning with tongs every 30 seconds to sear well on both sides; this takes 5 to 7 minutes for medium-rare. An instant-read thermometer inserted into the thickest part of the steak should read 128°F.

5. Transfer the steak to a wire rack and let rest for 5 minutes to allow the juices to recirculate. Transfer to a cutting board, cut the steak into thirds, and then slice against the grain into ¼-inch-thick slices. Arrange the steak on a serving platter. Season with fleur de sel and 6 turns of a peppermill. Serve with the remaining ½ cup sauce on the side.

Grilled Bone-In Prime Rib Eye

SERVES 4

A special-occasion dish for sure, a perfectly grilled rib eye is medium-rare from edge to edge and has a thick, crusty sear—a combination that sets this intensely beefy cut at the pinnacle of steaks. My method for grilling rib eye comes out of my fine-dining experience and the sous vide craze. I became determined to get that same succulent, evenly cooked result: a steak that is juicy and tender all the way through. Here's the key: You want to turn the meat often and rest it periodically during the grilling process to ensure even cooking. Also, because bone-in rib eye is big and fatty (I mean that in a good way), you need to watch out for the inevitable flare-ups from the beef fat dripping off the edges. When this happens (and it will), that's the time to close the lid or take the steak off the heat and let the flare-up subside before you return the meat to the heat of the grill. Lastly, when you turn the meat, take care to do it gently so the fat doesn't hit the grill grate with force and spit up. All this may feel like overkill, but the regimented cooking process helps the meat cook evenly all the way through. If you want to spice up the rib eye, rub it before grilling with any of the rubs in the Basics chapter (page 28). Serve with your favorite sides or the Smoked Fingerling Potatoes with Cipollini Onions (page 196).

2½ pound dry-aged prime bone-in rib eye steak (*côte de boeuf*), fat trimmed

Fine sea salt

Freshly ground black pepper

Vegetable oil, for greasing the grill

Fleur de sel

Extra-virgin olive oil, for drizzling on the steak

Snipped fresh flat-leaf parsley

Basque Vinegar (page 34), for serving

1. The night before you plan to cook the steak, pat it dry with paper towels and put it on a wire rack set inside a rimmed baking sheet. Chill, uncovered, in the refrigerator until about 2 hours before you want to grill your steak. Then remove it from the refrigerator and let sit on your counter so it comes up to room temperature. Season lightly with sea salt and pepper—you should see the seasoning on the meat.

2. Preheat a charcoal or gas grill to medium-high heat (400 to 450°F).

3. Take a few paper towels and fold them several times to make a thick square. Blot a small amount of vegetable oil on the paper towel,

recipe continues

then carefully and quickly wipe the hot grates of the grill. This will create a nonstick grilling surface.

4. Using tongs, hold the steak perpendicular to the grill and sear the fat cap-side down to render some of the fat. Lay the steak flat on the grill and sear, turning every 30 seconds for about 5 minutes total. (If flare-ups occur during the cooking process, close the lid in between turning the meat.) Transfer the steak to a rimmed baking sheet fitted with a wire rack insert and allow the meat to rest off the heat for 5 minutes. Close the lid while the steak rests to maintain the heat of the grill. The steak will not be done at this point, but resting this large cut of meat periodically helps control the internal temperature. Place the steak back on the grill and sear, turning every 30 seconds, until it begins to char, about 5 more minutes. Return the steak to rest on the wire rack for

5 minutes and close the lid again to maintain the heat. Return the steak to the grill and sear, turning every 30 seconds until nicely charred but not burned, about 5 more minutes. Finally, transfer the steak to the wire rack for its final rest for 5 minutes. The steak should be medium-rare with an even color and crispy fat. An instant-read thermometer inserted into the thickest part of the steak should read 130°F. Between all the grilling, flipping, and resting, the whole cooking process should take about 30 minutes.

5. Transfer the steak to a cutting board. Slicing parallel to the bone, cut the steak on a slight angle into ½-inch-thick slices. Transfer the sliced steak to a platter. Season the steak with fleur de sel and 6 turns of a peppermill. Drizzle the olive oil all over the top and garnish with parsley. Serve the vinegar in small dishes on the side for dipping.

Porcini-Dusted New York Strip

SERVES 4

There's no need to go to a steak house to enjoy a juicy New York strip steak, grilled to perfection! New York strip is a beautiful cut that has deep flavor and a melt-in-your mouth texture. I like to use dry-aged beef for this recipe—it's really in a class by itself. There are myriad chemical reactions that happen during the dry-aging process, but the result is that a lot of the water in the beef evaporates, which creates a more concentrated flavor in every bite. At the same time, the beef gets more tender. Dry-aged beef is typically more expensive but well worth it. But you can certainly use regular strip steaks here instead to fit your budget. Porcini adds an earthy-musky essence to the meat, especially if it's not dry aged. Serve with any of the sauces in the Basics chapter, such as J1 Steak Sauce (page 30) or Basque Vinegar (page 34). Loaded Yukon Gold Potatoes with Salted Butter, Crème Fraîche, Aged Gouda, and Chives (page 137) makes a perfect accompaniment.

Two 12- to 14-ounce boneless dry-aged prime New York strip steaks, about 1½ inches thick

½ cup Dried Porcini Rub (page 49)

Vegetable oil, for greasing the grill

Fine sea salt

Freshly ground black pepper

1. Put the steaks in a large baking dish and pat dry with paper towels. Sprinkle the porcini rub on both sides of the steaks. Cover and set aside in the refrigerator for at least 30 minutes or up to 2 hours to marinate so the flavors sink in. Take the meat out of the refrigerator about 30 minutes before grilling so that it comes up to room temperature.

2. Preheat a charcoal or gas grill to high heat (500°F).

3. Take a few paper towels and fold them several times to make a thick square. Blot a small amount of vegetable oil on the paper towel, then carefully and quickly wipe the hot grates of the grill. This will create a nonstick grilling surface. Season both sides of the steaks with salt.

4. Lay the steaks on the hot grill and sear for 6 minutes, turning them every 30 seconds to ensure even cooking. Transfer the steaks to a wire rack to rest for 5 minutes. Close the lid while the steaks rest to maintain the heat of the grill. Return the steaks to the grill and continue to cook, turning every 30 seconds, for 4 more minutes. Don't overcook; you want the steaks slightly charred on the outside and medium-rare inside. An instant-read thermometer inserted into the thickest part of the steak should read 130°F. Transfer to a wire rack, cover to keep warm, and let rest for 10 minutes to allow the juices to recirculate. Season with 6 turns of a peppermill. Serve the steaks cut on the bias into ½-inch-thick slices.

Chimichurri-Marinated Hanger Steak

SERVES 4

Hanger steak is one of the fuller-flavored and beefier cuts of meat. The Argentinean classic of hanger steak and chimichurri is among one of my favorite combos. I love the way the explosively tasty and herbaceous chimichurri sauce brings out the best in this cut. Very high heat is essential for this muscly piece of meat, but do take care not to grill the steak any longer than medium-rare doneness, or else you risk the chance of overcooking and the meat toughening up. While it might seem rigorous, turning the steaks every 30 seconds ensures that the inside of the meat is cooked evenly before the outside chars and potentially dries out. Serve with Corn Elote with Lime, Chile, Cilantro, and Cotija Cheese (page 148).

Two 1½-pound hanger steaks, trimmed, halved lengthwise, and center membrane removed

2 cups Smoked Paprika Chimichurri with Pickled Mustard Seeds (page 33)

Vegetable oil, for greasing the grill

2 teaspoons fine sea salt

Fleur de sel

Freshly ground black pepper

1. Lay the four pieces of hanger steak flat in a large baking dish and pour 1½ cups of the chimichurri evenly on top. Spread the sauce out to cover the surface, and then turn the meat over to coat both sides evenly. Set aside in the refrigerator to marinate for 2 to 6 hours, so the flavors can sink in a bit. You don't want to marinate the steak longer than that because the vinegar in the chimichurri will start to "cook" the meat. Take the meat out of the refrigerator about 30 minutes before grilling so that it comes up to room temperature.

2. Preheat a charcoal or gas grill to high heat (500°F).

3. Take a few paper towels and fold them several times to make a thick square. Blot a small amount of vegetable oil on the paper towel, then carefully and quickly wipe the hot grates of the grill. This will create a nonstick grilling surface.

4. Generously season the meat on all sides with the sea salt. Lay the steaks on the grill and cook, turning with tongs every 30 seconds, to sear on both sides. This takes 12 to 14 minutes total for medium-rare. An instant-read thermometer inserted into the thickest part of the steaks should read 130°F.

5. Transfer the steaks to a cutting board and let rest for 5 minutes to allow the juices to recirculate. Cut the steaks against the grain into ½-inch-thick slices and fan out on a serving platter. Season with fleur de sel and 6 turns of a peppermill. Serve with the remaining ½ cup sauce on the side.

Honey-Marinated Pork Chops with Pea Shoots

SERVES 4

One of the biggest problems that most people have with cooking pork chops is that they turn out dry and tough, with a shoe-leather texture. Pork is lean, prone to drying out, and easy to overcook. But if you flip the chops repeatedly—every 30 seconds or so—you can achieve a nice sear on the outside and an evenly cooked, moist interior.

I developed this simple marinade years ago when I was the chef at JiRaffe in Santa Monica, with my dear friend Raphael Lunetta. You might think vanilla and pork is an odd combination, but the fragrant spice lends itself beautifully to savory dishes, especially meat. If pea shoots are not available, substitute arugula.

1 lemongrass stalk, tough outer layer removed, smashed, and chopped into 2-inch pieces

1 whole vanilla bean, split and scraped, or ½ teaspoon pure vanilla extract

1 tablespoon fine sea salt, plus more for seasoning

1 tablespoon whole black peppercorns

1 tablespoon dried red pepper flakes

1 tablespoon fennel seeds

½ whole nutmeg, finely grated

1 tablespoon sherry vinegar

10 fresh thyme sprigs, leaves stripped from the stems

1 fresh rosemary sprig, leaves stripped from the stem

Finely grated zest of 1 orange

Finely grated zest of 1 lemon

¼ cup honey

2 cups extra-virgin olive oil, plus more to lightly coat the pea shoots and tendrils

Four 10- to 12-ounce bone-in pork rib chops, about 1-inch-thick and preferably free-range or Berkshire

Vegetable oil, for greasing the grill

1 cup pea shoots and tendrils or baby arugula

Juice of 1 lemon

Fleur de sel

Freshly ground black pepper

1. Prepare the marinade: In a medium mixing bowl, combine the lemongrass, vanilla seeds and pod, sea salt, peppercorns, red pepper flakes, fennel, nutmeg, vinegar, thyme, rosemary, orange zest, and lemon zest. Pour the honey in a microwave-safe container and microwave on medium power for 30 seconds to melt. Pour the liquefied honey into the mixing bowl and stir the ingredients together until evenly distributed. Slowly whisk in the olive oil.

2. Put the pork chops side by side in a baking dish and pat dry with paper towels. Pour the marinade over the pork, flipping them over to coat both sides. Cover with plastic wrap and refrigerate for at least 8 hours or preferably overnight to marinate, turning the pork over a couple of times. Take the meat out of the refrigerator about 30 minutes before grilling so that it comes up to room temperature.

3. Preheat a charcoal or gas grill to medium-high heat (400°F).

recipe continues

4. Take a few paper towels and fold them several times to make a thick square. Blot a small amount of vegetable oil on the paper towel, then carefully and quickly wipe the hot grates of the grill. This will create a nonstick grilling surface.

5. Remove the pork from the marinade and discard the marinade. Lightly pat the pork chops with paper towels to absorb any excess moisture. Season the pork chops on both sides generously with sea salt. Lay the pork chops on the hot grill and sear for a total of 15 minutes, turning them every 30 seconds to ensure even cooking. Don't overcook them; you want the chops slightly charred on the outside and pink in the center. An instant-read thermometer inserted into the thickest part of the meat should read 140°F. Transfer the pork chops to a wire rack, cover to keep warm, and let rest for 5 minutes to allow the juices to recirculate.

6. Meanwhile, prepare the garnish: In a large mixing bowl, toss together the pea shoots and tendrils with enough olive oil to lightly coat; drizzle with lemon juice and season with salt and pepper.

7. Transfer the pork chops to a cutting board. Cut the bones off each chop and then cut the meat into three even pieces. Arrange the bone and the meat decoratively among four plates. Sprinkle with fleur de sel and 2 turns of a peppermill. Garnish with the pea shoots and tendrils on top.

The Charcoal Bison Burger

SERVES 4

What makes a great burger? For me, it's the perfect ratio among meat, bun, and toppings. While I love buttery brioche or challah buns for my burgers, too much of a good thing tends to overpower the other elements. I like to cut out and discard the doughy center of the buns, leaving just the top dome and bottom base to ensure the bread does not upstage the burger itself. While ground beef reigns supreme in the burger world, bison (a.k.a. buffalo) meat is readily available in stores nowadays and is really lean with a rich, meaty flavor that bodes well for a burger. Since bison is low in fat, these burgers cook more quickly than beef and are best served medium-rare so they don't dry out.

1½ pounds ground bison

1 sweet onion, sliced into ¼-inch rounds

Vegetable oil, for greasing the grill

2 tablespoons extra-virgin olive oil

Fine sea salt

2 tablespoons mayonnaise

Freshly ground black pepper

4 slices white American cheese

4 large brioche or challah hamburger buns, top and bottom cut off and center discarded

Burger Sauce (recipe follows)

Butter or iceberg lettuce

Heirloom tomatoes, sliced ¼ inch thick

1. Using your hands, gently shape the ground bison into four patties, about 6 ounces each, 5 to 6 inches in diameter, and about 1 inch thick. Don't pack the meat too tightly—too much pressure will result in a tough, chewy burger. Place the formed burgers side by side on a pan and refrigerate to allow the patties to set for about 15 minutes.

2. Prepare the onions: Preheat a charcoal or gas grill to medium-high heat (400°F).

3. Take a few paper towels and fold them several times to make a thick square. Blot a small amount of vegetable oil on the paper towel, then carefully and quickly wipe the hot grates of the grill. This will create a nonstick grilling surface.

4. Lay the onion rounds flat on a rimmed baking sheet, drizzle with the olive oil, and season with salt. Grill the onions for 8 to 10 minutes, turning them over halfway through the cooking, until charred on both sides. Transfer the rounds to a cutting board and chop them into small pieces.

recipe continues

5. Brush both sides of the burgers lightly with mayonnaise and season generously with salt and pepper. Put the burgers on the grill and gently flatten them with the bottom of a spatula.

6. Grill the burgers for 3 minutes and then flip them over with a spatula. You want to flip the burgers only once; they should turn easily without sticking because of the fat in the mayo.

7. Sprinkle the burgers with the chopped charred onion, put a slice of cheese on top of each, and continue to grill the other side for 3 more minutes. An instant-read thermometer inserted into the center should read 140°F for medium-rare.

8. Transfer the grill rack with the same paper towel as before to clean the small charred pieces, then toast the hamburger buns cut-side down for 1 minute.

9. To build the burgers, spread 2 tablespoons of the burger sauce on the bottom bun, add a lettuce leaf and slice of tomato; season with salt and pepper. Top with the burgers, cheese-side up. Spread another 2 tablespoons of the sauce on the top bun and close.

Burger Sauce
MAKES ABOUT 1 CUP

This killer "secret" sauce is great on a burger or even French fries. A little bit different from the typical norm of mayo, ketchup, and relish, I came up with this custom concoction by playing around with what I had available in my pantry and fridge. The result is an insane balance of sweet, spicy, acidic, and savory.

1 cup mayonnaise

1½ tablespoons ketchup

1 tablespoon Worcestershire sauce

2 teaspoons Champagne vinegar

1½ teaspoons honey

1½ teaspoons grated fresh ginger

½ teaspoons wasabi paste

In a small mixing bowl, combine the mayonnaise, ketchup, Worcestershire, vinegar, honey, ginger, and wasabi. Whisk until smooth. The sauce may be stored, covered, in the refrigerator for up to 10 days.

Grilled Lamb Chops with Charred Eggplant Puree

SERVES 4

Succulent lamb and velvety eggplant is a classic Mediterranean pairing prominent in Greek, Italian, and French cuisines. Rosy in the center and charred on the outside, these little chops grill up in a flash and make a satisfying starter when friends walk in the door, a springtime appetizer for Easter dinner, or a light weeknight, casual dinner. You can easily double the recipe if you are serving more than four people. The coffee rub adds a caramel sweetness and nutty undertone to the delicious gamy flavor of the lamb. I often serve the lamb gyro-style, with the eggplant puree smeared on pita or charcoal flatbread (page 185) and lamb sliced on top. If serving with charcoal flatbread, it is best to omit the activated charcoal from the recipe so that the final presentation has a bit of color contrast.

8 lamb chops
(14 to 16 ounces total),
excess fat trimmed,
bones cleaned

¼ cup Coffee Rub
(page 53)

Vegetable oil, for greasing
the grill

Fine sea salt

Freshly ground black
pepper

Charred Eggplant Puree
(recipe follows), warm

4 pieces Charcoal
Flatbread (page 185)
or pita (optional)

1. Put the lamb chops in a large baking dish and pat dry with paper towels. Sprinkle the coffee rub on both sides of the lamb chops. Cover with plastic wrap and refrigerate for at least 30 minutes or up to 2 hours to marinate so that that the flavors sink in. Take the lamb out of the refrigerator about 30 minutes before grilling so that it comes up to room temperature.

2. Preheat a charcoal or gas grill to medium-high heat (400°F).

3. Take a few paper towels and fold them several times to make a thick square. Blot a small amount of vegetable oil on the paper towel, then carefully and quickly wipe the hot grates of the grill. This will create a nonstick grilling surface. Season the lamb chops on both sides generously with salt.

4. Lay the chops on the grill and sear for 3 to 4 minutes per side for medium-rare, turning them halfway through cooking to "mark" them. An instant-read thermometer inserted into the thickest part of the meat should read 130°F. Transfer the chops from the grill to a wire rack and let rest for 5 minutes to allow the juices to recirculate. Season with 6 turns of a peppermill. Serve with warm eggplant puree and charcoal flatbread on the side. Guests can build their own gyro at the table.

recipe continues

Charred Eggplant Puree

MAKES ABOUT 2 CUPS

You can make this lava-colored eggplant puree ahead of time. It's similar to baba ganoush, so you can use any leftovers as a dip with vegetable crudité. For a smoky flavor that will add depth to the finished dish, grill the eggplants on a very hot charcoal grill until they are completely black on both sides.

3 Chinese eggplants,
  2 eggplants with
  ends trimmed and
  sliced lengthwise into
  ½-inch-thick slices, and
  1 eggplant diced into
  ½-inch pieces

1 tablespoon vegetable oil

1 sweet onion,
  halved and sliced

Fine sea salt

1. Preheat a charcoal or gas grill to high heat (500°F).

2. Grill the eggplant slices until completely black and charred on both sides; turning every 5 minutes, for about 20 minutes.

3. Meanwhile, coat a medium saucepan with the vegetable oil and place over medium heat. Add the onion and salt. Cook and stir until completely tender, 3 to 4 minutes. Add the diced eggplant and season with another pinch of salt to release the natural moisture. Cook, stirring, until any liquid from the eggplant and onion has evaporated, 4 to 5 minutes. Add the charred eggplant, reduce to medium-low heat, and mix well to incorporate. Pour in ¾ cup water. Cook and stir until the liquid is reduced by half, about 5 minutes.

4. Working in batches if necessary, spoon the eggplant mixture into a blender, preferably a Vitamix, filling it no more than halfway. Puree on low speed for a few seconds, and then increase to medium-high speed until the sauce is completely smooth. Be sure to hold down the lid with a kitchen towel for safety. Add 1 tablespoon water at a time if the eggplant mixture is too thick to blend properly. Repeat with the remaining sauce until completely blended. Season again with a pinch of salt. Serve warm.

Grilled Tomato Bloody Mary

SERVES 4 TO 6

A thick, delicious, well-balanced Bloody Mary is a tried-and-true hangover cure. Spicy, savory, with a punch of acid and potent vodka, this popular weekend libation was a must when we launched brunch at Charcoal. Grilling fresh tomatoes concentrates their fruity flavor, making them super delicious in this Bloody Mary mix—which also makes an awesome dipping sauce for shrimp cocktail.

3 large heirloom or beefsteak tomatoes, cored and halved crosswise

Extra-virgin olive oil

Two 11½-ounce cans tomato juice

3 tablespoons grated fresh or prepared horseradish

2 tablespoons Worcestershire sauce

1 tablespoon green olive juice (reserve from the green olive garnish)

Juice of 3 limes

Juice of 1 lemon

1 tablespoon Tabasco sauce

1 tablespoon Sriracha or California Chili Sauce (page 40)

1 teaspoon caster (superfine) sugar

1 teaspoon fine sea salt

½ teaspoon freshly ground black pepper

1 celery stalk, ends trimmed, plus more for garnish

½ lime

Ice, for serving

Vodka, chilled in the freezer

Pepperoncini, large pitted green olives, and cocktail onions, skewered on toothpicks, for garnish

Charcoal Salt

¼ cup coarse salt

1 tablespoon celery salt

1 tablespoon activated charcoal powder (see Note, page 50)

1. Preheat a charcoal or gas grill to high heat (500°F). Chill 4 to 6 Collins glasses.

2. Rub the tomato skins well with olive oil to prevent them from sticking to the grill. Lay the tomato halves on the grill, cut-side down, and sear until you see grill marks, about 5 minutes. With tongs, turn the tomatoes over and grill the skin side for 3 to 4 minutes, until softened.

3. Transfer the tomatoes to a side platter to cool slightly. Peel off the skins and discard. Put the tomato flesh in a high-speed blender, preferably a Vitamix. Add the tomato juice, horseradish, Worcestershire, olive juice, lime juice, lemon juice, Tabasco, Sriracha, sugar, sea salt, pepper, and 1 celery stalk. Blend on high speed until completely smooth, about 1 minute. Pour into a pitcher and chill in the refrigerator for at least 2 hours or until ready to serve.

4. Prepare the charcoal salt: In a small mixing bowl, combine the salt, celery salt, and charcoal powder. Mix thoroughly until the color is even.

5. To serve, rub the ½ lime around the rims of the Collins glasses. Pour the charcoal salt on a plate and dip the wet rims into the salt to adhere. Turn the glasses upright, fill with ice, and pour about 2 ounces of vodka into each. Fill the glasses with the chilled Bloody Mary mix and stir gently with a bar spoon so that the vodka is distributed throughout. Put a piece of celery in each glass and lay a toothpick vegetable garnish across each rim.

Grilled Figs with Ricotta, Pomegranate Molasses, and Cacao Nibs

SERVES 4

Plump, sweet, and bursting with a delicate crunch from the tiny seeds, fresh figs are one of my all-time favorite fruits. In fact, the first thing I planted in my backyard in Venice was a Mission fig tree so I could harvest them myself. During the late summer to early fall, it bears so much fruit that I am always thinking of creative ways to use figs on my menus. When you are buying fresh figs for grilling, take care that they are not too soft or oozy, but just ripe, as you risk them collapsing into mush from the intense heat. Great for hot evenings, this simple summer dessert showcases the sexiness of this delicious fruit enlivened by tart pomegranate molasses, creamy ricotta, and chocolaty cacao nibs.

Vegetable oil, for greasing the grill

8 ripe large figs, such as Black Mission or Brown Turkey, halved lengthwise

¼ cup pomegranate molasses (see Note)

2 cups whole-milk ricotta

Extra-virgin olive oil, for drizzling on the grilled figs

Finely grated zest of 1 lemon

4 teaspoons cacao nibs

Ingredient Note: Pomegranate Molasses

Pomegranate molasses is a thick, reduced syrup of pomegranate juice that has a tart and fruity flavor. Colored a gorgeous, deep reddish purple, pomegranate molasses is commonly found in Mediterranean and Middle Eastern markets and keeps almost indefinitely in the refrigerator. If you can't find it, you can make it yourself. Pour 1 cup pure pomegranate juice into a small pot and heat over medium-low heat until the juice has reduced to ¼ cup and is thick and syrupy, about 15 minutes. Set aside to cool.

1. Preheat a charcoal or gas grill to medium-high heat (400 to 450°F).

2. Take a few paper towels and fold them several times to make a thick square. Blot a small amount of vegetable oil on the paper towel, then carefully and quickly wipe the hot grates of the grill. This will create a nonstick grilling surface.

3. In a medium mixing bowl, toss the fig halves with 1 tablespoon of the pomegranate molasses. Lay the figs on the hot grill, cut-side down, and sear them until you see grill marks, 2 to 3 minutes. With tongs, gently turn the figs over and grill the skin side for an additional 2 to 3 minutes, until softened and beginning to become jammy.

4. To serve, spoon ½ cup of the ricotta in the center of four plates and spread out with the back of a spoon. Arrange 4 fig halves on top, cut-side up. Drizzle the remaining 2 tablespoons pomegranate molasses among the four plates, add a light drizzle of olive oil, sprinkle with lemon zest all over the top, and garnish with 1 teaspoon of cacao nibs on each plate.

Charred Peach Bellini

SERVES 4 TO 6

This cocktail puts a new spin on the classic Italian bellini, which is traditionally made with peach puree and Prosecco sparkling wine. Here, I grill the peaches to add a smoky depth of flavor and a bit of viscosity to the drink. White or yellow peaches work well here. Depending on the ripeness of the peaches, you may wish to add more or less sugar to taste. You can make the peach puree ahead of time and refrigerate it for up to 1 day or freeze it for up to 1 month.

4 ripe peaches, halved and pitted

2 teaspoons extra-virgin olive oil

2 teaspoons caster (superfine) sugar

One 750-ml bottle chilled sparkling wine, such as Cava or Prosecco

1. Preheat a charcoal or gas grill to medium-high heat (400 to 450°F). Brush all sides of the peaches with the olive oil to prevent them from sticking to the grill.

2. Lay the peach halves on the hot grill, cut-side down, and sear until you see grill marks, 2 to 3 minutes. With tongs, gently turn the peaches over and grill the skin side for 3 to 4 minutes, until softened and aromatic.

3. Remove the peaches to a side plate to cool slightly. Transfer the grilled peaches to a high-speed blender, preferably a Vitamix, add the sugar, and puree until completely smooth. Depending on the ripeness of the peaches, you may need to add 1 to 2 tablespoons water to the blender to achieve a smooth puree. Pour the peach puree through a fine-mesh strainer into a bowl or measuring cup, working it through with the back of spoon to remove the skins. Chill the puree in the refrigerator for at least 1 hour or up to 1 day.

4. Spoon a couple tablespoons of the peach puree into champagne glasses and then top off with the sparkling wine. Stir gently to combine. Serve immediately.

IN THE COALS

The first time I experienced food cooked directly in the coals was years ago at a beautiful French home in the mountains above Nice. The palatial estate had a breathtaking courtyard, equipped with a custom-made built-in hearth where the host cooked steak right on the coals, with potatoes nestled in mounds of hardwood. The result was a meal to remember! Allowing the hot coals to come into direct contact with food creates a smoky, charred flavor that just can't be replicated by grilling. The char is robust and earthy but never too ashy or excessive.

Cooking directly in the coals—also known as campfire cooking, caveman-style, or dirty grilling—is nothing new. At an elemental level, it's the most primordial method of cooking since the beginning of mankind. Even in the '50s, President Eisenhower popularized the "Eisenhower Steak," as Ike liked to throw his filets atop a bed of fiery coals to sear. While a nice thick piece of meat is superb cooked in this manner, I strive to think outside the box. Two of our most-talked-about dishes on the Charcoal menu are actually vegetable dishes: Cabbage Baked in Embers with Yogurt, Sumac, and Lemon Zest (page 133) and Loaded Yukon Gold Potatoes with Salted Butter, Crème Fraîche, Aged Gouda, and Chive (page 137), and we cook them directly in the coals at the restaurant.

I discovered the astonishing range of coal cooking while testing out recipes at home in my Big Green Egg. Vegetables, as well as seafood, have a rustic depth and complexity when cooked in the coals that you'd never dream was possible.

One of the virtues of cooking in the embers, especially for people new to cooking with live fire, is that the food not only can, but should be burnt. Vegetables should be

cooked until the outside is as black as coal. The goal here is to not incinerate the food even though the heat is consistently 800 to 1,000°F, but instead to blacken the exterior and, in doing so, impart an incomparable smoke essence to the interior. This method of cooking is especially good if the foods come equipped with a sacrificial layer that can be stripped away before eating (i.e., corn, artichokes, and winter squash) since the cooking is done right down in the embers, and some exterior charring and ash adhesion comes with the territory. The fish skin and scales of the Whole Branzino Stuffed with Fennel and Lemon (page 159) also provides a protective layer, as does packing an ingredient into a salt crust shell (see Salt-Crusted Fennel with Olive-Tomato Vinaigrette, page 142) and Salt-Baked Whole Maine Lobster with Herbs and Lime (page 155).

There are basically two ways to go about roasting with this technique, and both require a fire that has burned a heap of hardwood coals long enough to be glowing red-hot. In one method, you bury the foods directly in the hot embers (Blackened Beets with Lemon-Scented Horseradish and Dill, page 146); in the other, you set the food directly on top (Roasted Radishes with Butter and Sea Salt, page 131).

You want to use only natural lump charcoal (not chemical-laden briquettes) in this method of cooking especially so that wood is the only ingredient touching what you eat. Lump is made of wood only, is all-natural and produces less ash, whereas briquettes are made up of a variety of things, may contain chemicals, and burn out more quickly. Also, never use lighter fluid—it is toxic and could get on your food.

Start by filling your barbecue or grill half-way up with charcoal. Using a rake, small shovel, or long-handled tongs, spread the coals evenly across the bottom grate. (I prefer regular metal kitchen tongs to barbecue tongs, which do not grip as well.) Always use a lot of coals when doing this type of cooking so that you never risk them burning out and needing to refeed the fire. You'll want to light the lump charcoal using fire starters or, if you prefer, a chimney starter. Put a fire starter in the center of the coals and three around in a clock formation. Keeping the bottom vent open, light the fire starters with a kitchen lighter. The coals should be ready to go in about 30 minutes and glowing red hot, depending on the size of your grill. If all of the coals are not entirely lit, use a rake, hoe, or shovel to mix them around. Tamp the coals down so you have an even layer. And most important, be sure to always wear sturdy closed-toe shoes and flexible fireproof gloves!

Allow the charcoal to really get going; you want it hot all over the coal bed. When the coals are glowing and have developed a thin layer of white ash on top, blow any accumulated ash off the coal bed by fanning them with a baking pan. A little wood ash is probably inevitable on your food, but it will be invisible and will not interfere with the flavor. If desired, you may use a dry pastry brush to wipe off any residual ash that may stick to the food.

When burying food, use a short shovel to dig out a few coals to make an indentation in the coal bed. Put the food in and carefully shovel hot coals from the perimeter to cover. Super important: Always use fireproof gloves and tongs when cooking in the coals! To extinguish and save your coals for another use, close the lid and vents to cut off the air supply.

Although it may sound challenging, cooking in the coals is frankly pretty simple if you follow commonsense fire-safety practices and the recipes accordingly. Most of all, with a little effort and attention, you can create intensely flavored meals that are guaranteed to please a crowd!

◇◇◇

Roasted Radishes with Butter and Sea Salt

SERVES 4 TO 6

J'adore radishes with butter and salt. It's simple in concept yet deliciously complex, comforting, and oh so French in flavor. When I was cooking in France, I'd visit my cousin's house in Normandy for Sunday supper. We'd always begin the classic way by grabbing a fresh radish by its stem, dunking it in good softened butter, and then rolling in a bit of fleur de sel. While radishes are typically eaten raw, roasting them mellows out the root vegetables' spicy bite while still retaining their refreshing crunch. At their peak in spring and thankfully available year-round, this underutilized vegetable makes a colorful hors d'oeuvre or snack to munch on. I don't discriminate when it comes to radishes, but the long red and white French breakfast variety are a bit milder than traditional radishes.

2 bunches large radishes, such as breakfast, rainbow, or red (about 20), tops on

8 tablespoons (1 stick) salted butter, such as Kerrygold or Beurre de Baratte, cold and cut into chunks

Finely grated zest and juice of ½ lemon, plus more zest for serving

1 teaspoon fine sea salt

Fleur de sel

Freshly ground black pepper

1. Put the radishes, along with their tops, in a colander and run under cool water to remove any dirt. Drain well.

2. Pull out a piece of heavy-duty aluminum foil big enough to hold half of the radishes and lay it out on a flat surface. Arrange 1 bunch of the radishes in the center of the foil. Put 4 tablespoons butter on top, plus half of the lemon zest and lemon juice, and sprinkle with ½ teaspoon of the sea salt. Gather the ends of the foil up over the radishes and crimp together to close. Take out another sheet of foil and put the sealed radish pouch on top, flipping it over so the seam side is down. For good measure, wrap again with another piece of foil to ensure that the radishes are fully sealed and so that ash does not creep inside and the butter does

not ooze out into the fire and flare up. Repeat the process with the remaining radishes, butter, lemon zest, lemon juice, and sea salt.

3. Remove the grill grate from a charcoal grill and build a hot fire with lump charcoal until red-hot, raking the coals to spread out evenly. Put on your fireproof gloves. Set the radish packets on top of the coals and cook for 12 minutes, flipping them over with tongs halfway through the cooking. The tops will be wilted and the radishes themselves should be tender but still firm in the center; check by piercing with a cake tester or paring knife.

4. Using tongs, transfer the radishes to a side platter and allow them to cool slightly, about 5 minutes. Gently rip open the pouches, being careful of the escaping steam. Sprinkle the radishes with fleur de sel, 3 to 4 turns of a peppermill, and grated lemon zest. Serve the radishes in the foil as a bowl for presentation. They may be served warm or at room temperature.

Cabbage Baked in Embers with Yogurt, Sumac, and Lemon Zest

SERVES 4

Who would have thought that the most popular dish on the Charcoal menu would be cabbage?! We bury a whole head of plain ol' green cabbage and cook it in blistering coals until the outer leaves are caramelized and give way to a soft, steamed interior. Because of its size and density, cabbage lends itself well to the smoldering embers of the fire, where it transforms and emerges juicy, smoky, and meaty. Trust me, even people who think they don't like cabbage—they've only had watery coleslaw or bland cabbage soup—go nuts for this addictive starter dish. Served warm, the charred cabbage leaves play off the coolness of the yogurt dipping sauce, which is fragrant with citrusy sumac and lemon. It's simple enough to add another head or two of cabbage for a gathering, and any leftovers you can slice into ribbons to top tacos. Be sure to try the yogurt sauce over any of your favorite grilled vegetables, such as eggplant, or use it as a dressing spooned over fresh tomato salad.

1 large head green cabbage (about 2 pounds)

Extra-virgin olive oil

Fine sea salt

1 cup plain whole-milk Greek yogurt

2 tablespoons finely chopped fresh chives

Finely grated zest of 1 lemon

Juice of ½ lemon

1 teaspoon sumac

1. Transfer the grill grate from a charcoal grill and build a hot fire with lump charcoal until red-hot. Rub the cabbage lightly with olive oil and season generously with salt, ensuring that all sides are well coated. Put on your fireproof gloves. Make a well in the center of the coals using a rake or shovel, and carefully add the cabbage. Use the rake or shovel to bury the cabbage completely by covering it with the surrounding hot coals. You may grill something on top at the same time if desired. Close the lid to keep the heat in and to prevent the charcoal from burning out too quickly. You want to maintain the temperature at about 400°F by adjusting the vents.

2. The cabbage should be completely charred and black on all sides and tender in the center in about 1 hour; check by piercing with a cake tester or paring knife. If it's not done, continue roasting in the coals for 5 more minutes. If you are preparing the cabbage ahead, wrap tightly in aluminum foil and keep it warm in a low oven.

3. In a small mixing bowl, combine the yogurt, chives, lemon zest, lemon juice, and sumac until smooth.

4. Cut the cabbage through the core into quarters. Cut the core out of each piece. Arrange the cabbage wedges on a serving platter and season lightly with salt. Rip off the cabbage leaves with your fingers and dip into the sauce.

Kabocha Squash Hummus

SERVES 6 TO 8

After tasting this silky squash hummus, you may never buy the store-bought stuff again. Kabocha is a Japanese squash with an almost chestnut flavor and sweetness that is boosted when you char it in the coals. If you can't find kabocha, substitute another winter squash, such as acorn, butternut, or delicata. Serve with Charcoal Flatbread (page 185) or pita, and pickled or roasted vegetables for a satisfying snack.

CHARCOAL

One 2½-pound kabocha squash

¾ cup cooked chickpeas

¼ cup plain Greek yogurt

3 tablespoons tahini

2 garlic cloves, minced after removing the germ (see Note, page 31)

Juice of 1 lemon

1 teaspoon fine sea salt, plus more if needed

1 teaspoon Piment d'Espelette (see Note, page 34) or cayenne

½ teaspoon ground coriander

½ cup pomegranate seeds

½ cup extra-virgin olive oil

4 fresh sage leaves, finely chopped

Charcoal Flatbread (page 185) or pita bread, quartered, for serving

1. Remove the grill grate from a charcoal grill and build a hot fire with lump charcoal until red-hot.

2. Put on your fireproof gloves. Make a well in the center of the coals using a rake or shovel, and carefully lay the squash in it.

3. Rotate the squash every 10 minutes so all of the sides sit directly in the coals to ensure even cooking. The squash is done when the skin is charred all over and it gives with light pressure, about 40 minutes. Gently remove the squash with tongs and set aside until cool enough to handle, about 30 minutes.

4. Using a serrated knife, cut off the crown of the squash and reserve it for serving. Using a tablespoon, scoop out and discard the seeds. Scrape out the flesh of the squash, getting as close to the skin as possible without puncturing it, and put it in the bowl of a food processor. Reserve the shell of the squash for serving. Add the chickpeas, yogurt, tahini, garlic, lemon juice, salt, Piment d'Espelette, and coriander. Pulse until a paste forms, pushing the ingredients down the sides of the bowl as needed, and then puree until completely smooth. While the motor is running, pour in the olive oil in a steady stream. If the hummus is too thick, add a few tablespoons of water at a time and puree to combine. Taste for seasonings and add salt if needed. Scoop the hummus into the reserved squash shell and fold in ¼ cup of the pomegranate seeds. Garnish with the sage and the remaining ¼ cup pomegranate seeds. Lean the squash lid against the hummus for serving. Serve with flatbread.

Loaded Yukon Gold Potatoes with Salted Butter, Crème Fraîche, Aged Gouda, and Chives

SERVES 4 TO 8

This is my fire-roasted take on the standard steak house baked potato. Yukon Gold potatoes are tossed directly into the coals until the skin is jet-black, and then topped with crème fraîche, sharp Gouda, and rich butter. It's important to purchase the biggest potatoes you can find at your local market; the varieties that we source for the restaurant are about the size of Mr. Potato Head! Feel free to substitute russet or Idaho potatoes for the Yukon if they're larger. Depending upon the size and the heat of your fire, the potatoes will be done in anywhere from 40 to 50 minutes. The skin should be completely black and the inside tender. This is one of our menu staples that people can't get enough of and come back for time and time again. The loaded potatoes go great with any of the grilled meats in the book.

4 large Yukon Gold or russet potatoes (12 to 16 ounces each), scrubbed

8 tablespoons (1 stick) salted butter, such as Kerrygold or Beurre de Baratte

8 generous tablespoons crème fraîche

4 ounces aged Gouda cheese, shredded (about 1½ cups)

8 tablespoons finely chopped fresh chives

1. Remove the grill grate from a charcoal grill and build a hot fire with lump charcoal until red-hot. Put on your fireproof gloves. Make a well in the center of the coals using a rake or shovel and add the potatoes. Use the rake or shovel to bury the potatoes completely by covering them with the surrounding hot coals. You may grill something on top at the same time if desired. Close the lid to keep the heat in and prevent the charcoal from burning out too quickly. You want to maintain the temperature at about 400°F by adjusting the vents. The potatoes should be completely charred and black on all sides and tender in the center in about 40 minutes, depending on their size; check them by piercing with a cake tester or paring knife. If not done, continue roasting in the coals for 5 more minutes. If you are preparing the potatoes ahead, wrap them tightly in aluminum foil and keep them warm in a low oven.

2. Working with one potato at a time, cut a slit lengthwise down the center and press the ends in toward each other to open it up. Add 2 tablespoons of butter and fluff with a fork so the butter melts into the flesh of the potato. Spoon 2 tablespoons of the crème fraîche on top. Top with 1 ounce of the Gouda and 2 tablespoons of the chives. Repeat with the remaining potatoes.

VARIATION:

These loaded potatoes make a super-satisfying brunch dish with the addition of crumbled bacon and a runny poached egg. After you fluff the butter into the potato, sprinkle with crumbled crisp bacon, then a poached egg. Finish with the crème fraîche, Gouda, and chopped chives

Coal-Roasted Carrots with Ricotta, Herbs, and Black Pepper Honey

SERVES 4 TO 6

Few cooking methods do more to bring out a vegetable's natural sweetness than fire does to carrots. The high, dry heat caramelizes the natural sugars and the charring imparts a pleasantly bitter flavor to counteract the carrots' sweetness. Black pepper and honey is one of my favorite duos and the perfect foil for fire-kissed carrots. Tangy and sweet, a final toss shellacs the carrots in a glistening glaze that ties it all together. To move the carrots in and out of the fire easily, you'll need a vegetable grill basket. The carrots will blacken in spots, so if you are using purple carrots, take care not to peel off too much of the dark flesh along with the charred bits.

2 pounds small rainbow carrots (about 24), tops trimmed

Extra-virgin olive oil

Fine sea salt

½ cup honey

1 tablespoon whole black peppercorns, coarsely cracked with the back of a heavy skillet or mallet

2 tablespoons unsalted butter

½ cup whole-milk ricotta, preferably sheep's milk

1 tablespoon whole milk

1 tablespoon Basque Vinegar (page 34) or apple cider vinegar

4 small fresh basil leaves, cut into small pieces with scissors

2 fresh flat-leaf parsley sprigs, leaves picked from the stems

2 fresh chives, cut into ½-inch pieces with scissors

2 small fresh opal basil leaves, cut into small pieces with scissors (optional)

Fleur de sel

Freshly ground black pepper

1. Remove the grill grate from a charcoal grill and build a hot fire with lump charcoal until red-hot. Put the carrots in a large mixing bowl and coat lightly with olive oil and season generously with salt, tossing to coat. Arrange the carrots in a grill basket in an even layer. Put on your fireproof gloves. Lay the grill basket with the carrots on top of the coals and, using a rake or shovel, carefully cover them with the surrounding hot coals so they are completely buried. The carrots should be charred and black in spots and slightly tender in the center in 5 to 6 minutes; check by piercing with a cake tester or paring knife.

2. Using tongs, carefully transfer the carrots to a bowl, cover with plastic wrap, and let them sweat for about 10 minutes to loosen their skins. Once the carrots are cool enough to handle, rub off the charred skins with paper towels. They don't have to be perfect; if a few burned bits are left on the carrots, don't sweat it. Set aside at room temperature while preparing the rest of the dish.

recipe continues

3. Place the honey and cracked pepper in a small saucepan and heat over medium-low heat until the mixture begins to bubble and turn a dark amber color, about 4 minutes. Add 2 teaspoons water and mix until well combined and the honey thins out slightly. Whisk in the butter until melted and continue to cook and whisk until the honey mixture is emulsified, about 5 minutes. Remove from the heat and cover to keep warm.

4. In a small mixing bowl, mix the ricotta and milk to loosen until it resembles small-curd cottage cheese. Set aside at room temperature.

5. Coat a large sauté pan with olive oil and heat over medium heat. Lay the carrots in the pan and toss until heated through, about 2 minutes. Once the carrots are hot, pour in the pepper honey and continue to cook and toss until the carrots are shiny and glazed, about 5 minutes. Drizzle with the vinegar and toss to coat.

6. To serve, mound the ricotta in the center of a serving bowl and arrange the glazed carrots around it. Sprinkle with the basil, parsley, chives, and opal basil, if using. Season with fleur de sel and 3 turns of a peppermill. Finish with a drizzle of olive oil over the top.

Salt-Crusted Fennel with Olive-Tomato Vinaigrette

SERVES 4 TO 6

While I love cooking fresh seafood in salt crust (Salt-Baked Whole Maine Lobster with Herbs and Lime, on page 155, is a perfect main course to serve with this vegetable side), fennel also beautifully lends itself to this cooking method. The licorice-like vegetable absorbs a bit of the surrounding salt, making it extra tender without browning. Topped with chunky Mediterranean vinaigrette, it's not a deal breaker if you choose to omit the coffee rub in the crust, but it will take the fennel to another level. Leftover fennel tops can be used in Whole Branzino Stuffed with Fennel and Lemon (page 159). You'll need cheesecloth to hold the salt crust in place around the fennel so it can harden up in the coals without damage.

2 large heirloom tomatoes

12 pitted Niçoise olives, finely chopped

4 large fresh mint leaves, cut into chiffonade

1 shallot, minced

1 tablespoon capers, drained

1 tablespoon Champagne vinegar

Finely grated zest and juice of ½ orange

½ teaspoon fine sea salt

¼ cup extra-virgin olive oil

6 cups kosher salt, preferably Diamond

¼ cup Coffee Rub (page 53) (optional)

½ cup egg whites (from 4 large eggs)

3 large fennel bulbs, tops removed

1. Cut off the four sides of the tomatoes to make a square to remove the seeds and peel. Cut the tomatoes into ¼-inch dice and put in a medium mixing bowl. Add the olives, mint, shallot, capers, vinegar, orange zest, orange juice, and sea salt. Fold the ingredients together gently but thoroughly. Mix in the olive oil until fully incorporated. You should have about 2½ cups. The vinaigrette can be made 1 day ahead before serving and keeps for 3 days covered in the refrigerator.

2. In a large mixing bowl, combine the kosher salt and coffee rub, if using. Gradually pour in the egg whites and mix with a rubber spatula. The salt mixture should be firm and wet and hold together when you squeeze it together in your hand (like the texture of making a sand castle at the beach).

3. Lay out a piece of cheesecloth (big enough to cover a fennel bulb) in a small bowl. Spread a mound of the salt mixture in the center of the cheesecloth, about ½ inch thick. Stand

recipe continues

a fennel bulb upright on the salt and cover with enough of the salt mixture to completely cover. Gather the four ends of the cheesecloth up over the fennel and twist the top together to tighten, while at the same time using your hands to press the salt mixture evenly around the fennel. Tie the cheesecloth with kitchen twine and double knot it to secure. Transfer the wrapped fennel to a side platter and repeat the process with the remaining fennel bulbs and salt mixture.

4. Remove the grill grate from a charcoal grill and build a hot fire with lump charcoal until red-hot, raking the coals to spread out evenly. Put on your fireproof gloves. Lay the fennel directly in the coals and cook for 25 minutes, flipping over halfway through the cooking with tongs, until the salt crust is completely hard and the cheesecloth is singed in spots.

5. Using tongs, carefully transfer the fennel to a cutting board and allow to cool slightly for 5 minutes. Crack the salt crust with a chef's knife, being careful of the escaping steam. Pull off the pieces of the crust with your hands. Cut the fennel bulbs into wedges and arrange faceup on a serving platter. Spoon several tablespoons of the vinaigrette on and around the fennel and serve the remaining vinaigrette on the side.

Blackened Beets
with Lemon-Scented Horseradish and Dill

SERVES 4 TO 6

Beets have come a long way since I was a kid. If you grew up on canned beets, it's understandable why you hate them. When I moved to France as a young cook, I discovered that beets were notably featured at many fine restaurants, as well as at "peasant-style" countryside dinners, and I became completely obsessed with all the ways they were deliciously prepared. Roasting beets gives them a deep, earthy taste that can't be accomplished any other way. Topped with the classic combo of zingy horseradish cream and fresh dill, these beets will convince even the biggest haters of their virtue. If you like a bit more heat, soak the fresh horseradish in cool water for an hour or two to intensify its spiciness in the sauce. There are many varieties of beets available at the market these days. Have fun and get different colors for a visually striking dish. If you are using dark red beets, remember to wrap and roast them separately so you don't discolor the lighter-colored ones.

½ cup crème fraîche or sour cream

¼ cup grated fresh or prepared horseradish (see Headnote)

2 tablespoons coarsely chopped fresh dill, plus more for garnish

Finely grated zest and juice of 1 lemon

⅛ teaspoon Piment d'Espelette (see Note, page 34) or cayenne

Fine sea salt

12 medium rainbow beets, such as red, golden, and striped (2 to 3 bunches), 1½ to 2 inches in diameter, unpeeled and rinsed, tops reserved, and stems trimmed

¼ cup extra-virgin olive oil, plus more for drizzling

¼ cup Champagne vinegar

Freshly ground black pepper

Fleur de sel

1. In a small mixing bowl, combine the crème fraîche, horseradish, dill, lemon zest, lemon juice, Piment d'Espelette, and a pinch of salt. Mix well with a small whisk until smooth. Cover and chill in the refrigerator for at least 1 hour or up to overnight so the flavors come together.

2. If you are using multiple-colored beets, you want to wrap the red ones separately from the others to avoid staining. Pull out a piece of aluminum foil big enough to hold each color variety of beets and lay out on a flat surface. Stack 3 to 4 of the beet leaves in the center of the foil, overlapping them slightly—be sure to use the leaves with the corresponding colored beet. Lay the beets on top of the leaves, drizzle with olive oil, and season with salt. Cover the beets with the remaining leaves. Gather the ends of the foil up over the beets and crimp together to close. Take out another sheet of foil for each pouch and put the sealed beets on top, flipping them over so the seam side

is down. Double wrapping the beets in foil ensures that they are fully sealed so ash does not creep inside.

3. Remove the grill grate from a charcoal grill and build a hot fire with lump charcoal until red-hot. Put on your fireproof gloves. Make a well in the center of the coals using a rake or shovel and add the beet packets. Use the rake or shovel to bury the beets completely by covering them with the surrounding hot coals. Close the lid to keep the heat in and prevent the charcoal from burning out too quickly. Cook for 30 minutes. The beets should be tender in the center; check by piercing with a cake tester or paring knife. If they are not done, continue roasting them in the coals for 2 more minutes.

4. Using tongs, transfer the beets to a side platter and allow to cool slightly for 5 minutes. Gently rip open the pouches, being careful of the escaping steam. Once the beets are cool enough to handle, discard the beet greens and rub off the skins with paper towels. If you are using red beets, it's wise to wear rubber gloves and put down a piece of wax paper on your cutting board, so you don't stain everything red! Cut the beets in half or quarters, depending on their size. Put the beets in mixing bowls. Keep the red beets in a separate bowl from the golden and striped, if using, so they don't bleed.

5. In a small bowl or liquid measuring cup, mix the vinegar, 2 tablespoons water, and the remaining ¼ cup of olive oil. Pour the mixture over the beets, dividing if necessary between the colors. Season lightly with sea salt and 4 turns of a peppermill.

6. In a wide, shallow bowl or serving platter, arrange the beets by color and drizzle each with any remaining liquid from each bowl, keeping true to each color. Garnish with chopped dill and season with fleur de sel. Serve the sauce on the side.

Corn Elote with Lime, Chile, Cilantro, and Cotija Cheese

SERVES 4

A few times a year, my teenage buddies that I grew up with and I all get together for a reunion surfing trip. Camping out on the beach, we build a fire together and cook whatever we can get our hands on over open flame. No matter what else we make, roasted corn on the cob is always on the menu. A Mexican treasure, whole roasted corn slathered in creamy chili, lime, and salty cheese is a street food staple that needs no embellishment. Showcase this universal side dish come summertime, when corn is at its peak.

CHARCOAL

4 ears fresh corn, in husk

¼ cup mayonnaise

2 tablespoons Mexican crema fresca or sour cream

1 teaspoon ancho chili powder, plus more if you like it spicy

Juice of ½ lime

1 cup crumbled Cotija cheese

Tajín seasoning

¼ cup chopped fresh cilantro

Lime wedges, for serving (optional)

1. Gently pull the husks away from corn (do not detach from the cob) and remove the silk strands. Put the husks back in place to cover the corn kernels and secure with kitchen string so ash does not get inside. Put the corn in a large, wide pot or bucket and cover with cold water; put a pan or plate on top to keep the corn submerged in the water. Soak the corn for 30 minutes to 1 hour; this will prevent the husks from burning and the corn from drying out.

2. Meanwhile, in a small mixing bowl, mix together the mayonnaise, crema, chili powder, and lime juice. Spread the Cotija out on a flat plate. Set aside while roasting the corn.

3. Remove the grill grate from a charcoal grill and build a hot fire with lump charcoal until red-hot, raking the coals to spread out evenly. Put on your fireproof gloves. Nestle the corn in the coals in a single layer. Roast the corn for 15 to 20 minutes, turning with tongs periodically. The husks should be charred in spots and some of the kernels should blacken.

4. Pull the husks down to the stem of the corn and gather them together to use them as a handle. Slather the hot corn with the mayonnaise mixture and roll in the Cotija to completely cover. Sprinkle with Tajín and cilantro. Serve with lime wedges, if desired.

Charred Artichokes with Lemon Aioli

SERVES 4 TO 6

Inspired by trips to Spain and Italy, I love the complex simplicity of sticking artichokes in intense heat and waiting for the ultimate magic to happen. Fire-roasted artichokes, with their crackling crisp leaves and hauntingly smoky flavor, get the Mediterranean treatment laden with fresh herbs, pungent garlic, and dried red pepper flakes. A compelling hands-on appetizer, grilling intensifies artichoke's unique flavor, and dipping the charred leaves into luscious lemony aioli takes the dish over the top—in a good way!

½ cup extra-virgin olive oil

4 large fresh basil leaves, chopped

4 fresh flat-leaf parsley sprigs, chopped

2 garlic cloves, minced after removing the germ (see Note, page 31)

½ shallot, minced

1 teaspoon fine sea salt

½ teaspoon dried red pepper flakes

4 large whole artichokes (about 2 pounds total)

Fleur de sel

Freshly ground black pepper

Lemon Aioli (recipe follows), for serving

1. In a small mixing bowl, combine the olive oil, basil, parsley, garlic, shallot, salt, and red pepper flakes. Set aside and keep at room temperature.

2. Cut off the stems at the bases of the artichokes so they are flat and the artichokes stand upright. Cut ½ inch off the crown of each artichoke. Open the artichokes from the top, gently prying the leaves apart to expose the center choke. Spoon a couple of tablespoons of the oil-herb mixture inside the cavity of each artichoke.

3. Remove the grill grate from a charcoal grill and build a hot fire with lump charcoal until red-hot, raking the coals to spread out evenly. Put on your fireproof gloves. Using tongs, stand the artichokes upright in the coals. Cook the artichokes for 20 to 25 minutes, until the outer leaves are charred. Close the lid and continue to cook for 10 to 15 minutes more, until the leaves pull out easily and the heart is tender. Check by piercing with a cake tester or paring knife.

4. Using tongs, carefully transfer the artichokes to a cutting board and allow to cool slightly for 5 minutes. Cut the artichokes into quarters and remove any remaining choke with a spoon. Arrange faceup on a serving platter. Sprinkle with fleur de sel and 6 to 8 turns of a peppermill. Serve with lemon aioli.

recipe continues

Lemon Aioli

MAKES ABOUT 1 CUP

Aioli is chef code for jazzed-up mayo. In addition to making a great dip for the charred artichokes, try it on grilled fish or even as a savory sandwich spread.

1 cup mayonnaise

1 tablespoon Dijon mustard

Juice of 1 lemon, plus more as needed

¼ cup finely chopped fresh flat-leaf parsley leaves

2 garlic cloves, minced after removing the germ (see Note, page 31)

3 tablespoons extra-virgin olive oil

Fine sea salt

Piment d'Espelette (see Note, page 34) or cayenne

Combine the mayonnaise, mustard, lemon juice, parsley, and garlic in a small bowl. Gently whisk until the ingredients are combined. Slowly drizzle in the olive oil while whisking until the aioli is thickened and smooth; season with salt and Piment d'Espelette. Cover and chill for at least 30 minutes. The flavor of the aioli gets better as it sits. Aioli can be made 1 day ahead and keeps in the refrigerator for up to 1 week. Stir in 1 tablespoon water or lemon juice to thin out if needed.

Salt-Baked Whole Main Lobster with Herbs and Lime

SERVES 2

Baking in salt involves nothing more than burying food in a sandlike mixture of salt and egg white to form a crust. Salt naturally insulates the food, cooking it gently and evenly. When the dish comes out of the coals, you crack open the hardened, black salt shell to unearth a moist, evenly cooked, and fragrant buried treasure. Serving a whole lobster is impressive on its own, but crusting it in salt and cooking it over fiery coals makes for a dramatic presentation and takes it to another level (plus it's not difficult to pull off). The result is succulent and sweet meat with a subtle, smoky flavor. The only downside to this salt-baked cooking method is that it's virtually impossible to check for doneness (given the hard shell), so do follow the times given in the recipe. You'll need cheesecloth to hold the salt crust in place around the lobster so it can harden up in the coals without damage. This recipe is totally scalable; feel free to double or triple for more people.

One (1½ pound) live Maine lobster

½ cup white vinegar

8 cups plus 1 tablespoon kosher salt, preferably Diamond

1 cup egg whites (from 8 large eggs)

Fleur de sel

Piment d'Espelette (see Note, page 34) or cayenne

4 fresh chives, finely chopped

3 fresh flat-leaf parsley sprigs, coarsely chopped

2 fresh tarragon sprigs, leaves coarsely chopped

Extra-virgin olive oil, for drizzling

1 lime, halved

1. Fill a large stockpot three-quarters of the way with water and add the vinegar and 1 tablespoon of the kosher salt. Bring to a rapid boil over medium-high heat. (Adding vinegar to the water is a chef trick to help the lobster meat from sticking to its shell. Trust me!)

2. Prepare an ice bath by filling a large bowl halfway with water and adding a tray of ice cubes. Carefully ease the lobster into the boiling water and cook for 1 minute. Using tongs, carefully transfer the lobster from the pot and plunge it into the ice bath. Chill the lobster in the ice water until completely cool, 2 to 3 minutes. Transfer the lobster to a cutting board and cut off the antennas and legs with kitchen shears.

recipe continues

3. Put the remaining 8 cups salt in a large mixing bowl, gradually pour in the egg whites, and mix with a rubber spatula. The salt mixture should be firm and wet and hold together when you squeeze it together in your hand (like the texture of making a sand castle at the beach).

4. Lay out a large piece of cheesecloth (about an 18-inch square) on a baking sheet. Spread a layer of the salt mixture down the center of the cheesecloth, a little longer than the length of the lobster and about ½ inch thick. Lay the lobster on the salt, belly-side down. Using your hands, mound the remaining salt on top of the lobster to cover completely. Carefully roll up the lobster in the cheesecloth, tucking in the sides to form a neat package, then continue rolling until it is completely wrapped in the cheesecloth. Cut another large piece of cheesecloth and wrap another layer around the lobster to ensure that the salt crust stays in place.

5. Remove the grill grate from a charcoal grill and build a hot fire with lump charcoal until red-hot, raking the coals to spread out evenly.

Put on your fireproof gloves. Place the lobster directly in the coals, back-side down. Cook for 6 minutes, and then carefully flip over with tongs and cook for another 6 minutes, until the exterior is black.

6. Using tongs, carefully transfer the lobster to a cutting board and allow to cool slightly for 10 minutes.

7. Hold the lobster in place using tongs or put on barbecue gloves to hold it steady. Crack the salt crust with a chef's knife, being careful of the escaping steam. Pull off the pieces of the crust with your hands or two spoons.

8. Split the lobster in half down the middle and put on a serving platter, meat-side up. Sprinkle lightly with fleur de sel and Piment d'Espelette. Mix the chives, parsley, and tarragon together in a small bowl and sprinkle over the lobster. Drizzle with olive oil and squeeze with lime. Serve with seafood forks or nutcrackers.

Whole Branzino Stuffed with Fennel and Lemon

SERVES 4

Cooking a whole fish makes an awesome presentation, and the taste of the flesh cooked on the bone is uniquely deep and luscious. Commonly roasted or grilled, branzino is a Mediterranean favorite that I relish cooking directly on scorching coals for super-intense flavor. Take note when buying the whole fish: You want to keep the scales on, as they create a barrier to protect the delicate meat from drying out. In the last half of cooking, it's best to put the lid on the grill to guarantee that the inside of the fish is cooked just right all of the way through. While cooking an entire whole fish might seem scary to master, the truth is that it's shockingly modest to prepare, but you definitely get the wow factor. Serve with Salt-Crusted Fennel with Olive-Tomato Vinaigrette (page 142) or thinly slice the fennel bulb leftover from the tops in the stuffing and toss with wild arugula, a spritz of lemon, good olive oil, and salt and pepper. If you can't get your hands on branzino, any firm white-fleshed fish may be substituted, such as snapper or sea bass. Carving is easy with a knife and a tablespoon if you want to show off skills tableside.

Two 1½-pound whole Branzino (*loup de mer*) or striped bass, head, tail, and scales on, fins removed, and gutted

Fine sea salt and freshly ground black pepper

3 lemons

1 fennel bulb, top and fronds only, coarsely chopped

Extra-virgin olive oil

Fleur de sel

1. Season the insides of the fish generously with salt and pepper. Cut one of the lemons in half lengthwise and slice into half-moons. Stuff the cavities of the fish with the lemon slices and fennel. Secure the openings with 4 or 5 toothpicks to keep the lemon and fennel from falling out of the fish.

2. Remove the grill grate from a charcoal grill and build a hot fire with lump charcoal until red-hot, raking the coals to spread out evenly. Put on your fireproof gloves. Using tongs, place the fish directly on the coals and cook for 6 minutes. Carefully flip the fish over with both a spatula and tongs and cover with the lid. Keep the vents open and continue to cook for 6 more minutes. Using a flat spatula, carefully transfer the fish to a cutting board and let rest for 10 minutes. The fish, thanks to the bones, can rest for a bit and will remain hot and moist while you finish the dish. While the

recipe continues

fish is resting, cut the remaining lemons in half crosswise and put the grate back on top of the charcoal grill. Grill the lemon halves facedown for 4 minutes, until charred and juicy.

3. To fillet the fish, lay the fish on a cutting board or platter on its side and pull out the toothpicks. Peel off the blackened skin from the body of the fish with a tablespoon or your fingers (you may want to wear kitchen gloves to prevent black bits from digging under your fingernails). Flip the fish over and remove the skin on the other side. Discard all of the charred skin; you don't want any black bits to taint the beautiful branzino meat.

4. Using a thin, sharp knife, cut along the top of the fish through the skin, along where the fin used to be. Make an incision below the head, where the neck would be, and do the same at the tail end, making an incision where the tail begins on the body.

5. Now, gently run the knife lengthwise down the middle of the fish, following the natural division between the top and bottom of the spine. Gently work the flesh free from the top portion and flip the fillet off the bottom portion of the fish, away from the center skeleton bone. Do the same with the belly meat on the bottom portion of the fish. Pull out any little bones in the fillets with your fingers. Working from the tail end, lift the skeleton up toward the head, revealing the bottom fillet—the head should come off with it in one big piece. Clean out the fennel and lemon stuffing in the bottom fillet and remove any pin bones. Display the fish fillets on a serving platter, drizzle with olive oil, season with fleur de sel, and squeeze the grilled lemon on top tableside.

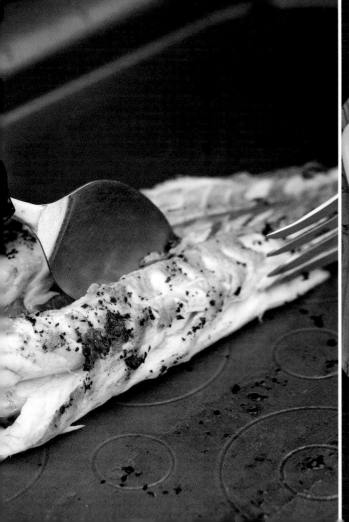

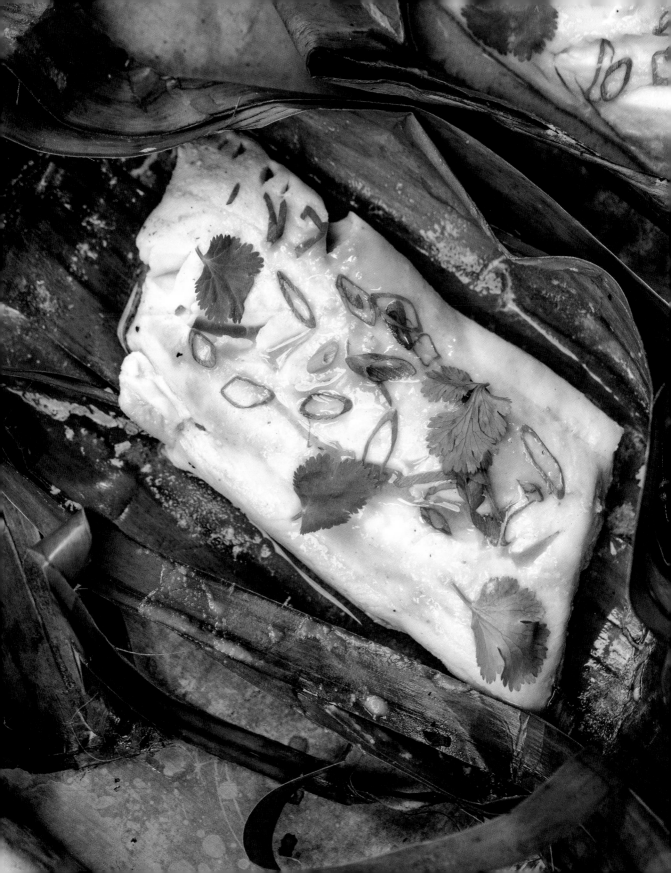

Black Cod Wrapped in Banana Leaf with Honey, Dijon, and Miso

SERVES 4

Black cod is actually not truly cod at all, but sablefish. To add to the confusion, in some markets, the white fish is also referred to as "butterfish," dubbed so for its rich, creamy texture. Black cod is caught all along the cold depths off the Pacific Coast, and the oily nature of the flesh stands up very well to high heat. In my spin on chef Nobu Matsuhisa's signature dish, Black Cod in Miso, I add sweet and spicy honey-mustard to embrace my French heritage and balance out the salinity of miso paste. With only a handful of ingredients, the marinade is a snap to prepare, while delivering big on flavor and a striking presentation. The vital ingredient in this dish is the banana leaves, which you can often find in the frozen section of Latin and Asian markets. Wrapping the fish in banana leaves gently cooks it—the leaves release water, trap steam, and ultimately protect their prized contents from drying out as they cook. The smoke of fire cooking is a natural complement to the grassy, floral flavor the banana leaf imparts. And when you unwrap a banana leaf parcel, it releases a wonderful tropical aroma. Serve with steamed jasmine rice and sautéed Asian greens, such as tatsoi with shiitake mushrooms.

½ cup Dijon mustard

½ cup honey

¼ cup white miso paste

¼ cup freshly squeezed lemon juice (about 2 lemons)

Four 6-ounce skinless black cod fillets (sablefish), ½ inch thick, pin bones removed

4 banana leaves, each about 12 inches square, thawed if frozen

2 scallions (green parts only), sliced on a bias, for serving

4 fresh cilantro sprigs, leaves picked from stems, for serving

1. In a medium mixing bowl, whisk together the mustard, honey, miso, and lemon juice until smooth. Lay the cod fillets side by side in a baking dish, pour the marinade over the fish, and then flip over a couple of times, so both sides are well coated. Cover and marinate the cod in the refrigerator for 6 hours or up to overnight.

2. Remove the grill grate from a charcoal grill and build a hot fire with lump charcoal until red-hot, raking the coals to spread out evenly. To make the banana leaves more pliable for wrapping the fish, heat each one over the coals for about 30 seconds, holding the leaves one by one with long-handled tongs, until the leaves are warmed and softened and become slightly shiny.

recipe continues

163

3. To wrap the fish, lay a banana leaf on a work surface and set a fish fillet on the lower half, with the grains of the leaf running parallel. Fold the banana leaf up over the fish and continue to roll until fully enclosed. Fold the two sides of the banana leaf under so you have a rectangle. Pull out a 12-inch piece of aluminum foil and roll up the banana leaf–wrapped cod in the foil exactly the same way into a package—the foil will protect the leaves from burning. Repeat the process with the remaining banana leaves and black cod.

4. Put on your fireproof gloves. Lay the fish packets directly on the coals and cook for 6 minutes, carefully turning halfway through cooking with tongs. Transfer the fish packets to a platter or cutting board to rest for 5 minutes. The fish should be firm and flaky and opaque in the center. Remove the foil and discard.

5. Put each banana leaf–wrapped cod on a dinner plate, and let guests unwrap their own parcel and breathe in the aromatic steam at the table. Serve sliced scallions and cilantro leaves on the side for topping.

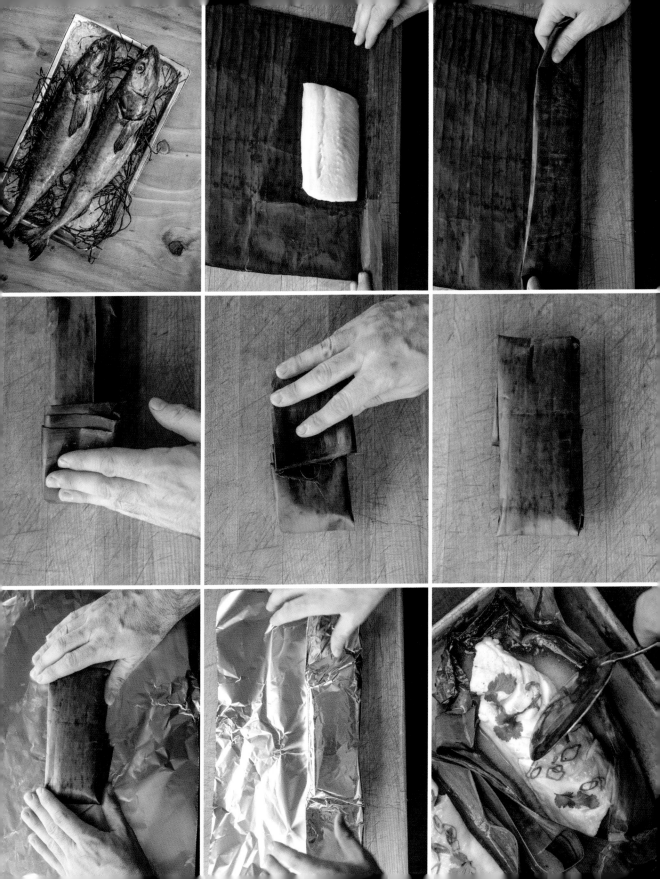

Eisenhower Sausage and Peppers Hero

SERVES 4

Dwight Eisenhower is known not only for serving as the thirty-fourth president of the United States. He's also notable for his method of cooking steak directly on a bed of blazing coals. Fittingly known as "Eisenhower Steak," his technique of setting food right on the fire is the foundation of this chapter and part of the magic that makes Charcoal so unique. I thought it would be fun to do my own spin on the method and re-create a classic Italian sandwich. Sausage, peppers, and onions roasted in the coals take this street-food favorite to another level. Poblano peppers innately have a smoky flavor and lack the bitterness of the green peppers typically used. If you are throwing a backyard party, you can easily double the recipe.

1 large poblano pepper

1 red bell pepper

1 yellow bell pepper

1 sweet onion, unpeeled

1 tablespoon balsamic vinegar

1 tablespoon extra-virgin olive oil

Fine sea salt and freshly ground black pepper

4 fresh Italian sausages, sweet or hot (about 1 pound)

4 sourdough sandwich rolls or 1 large baguette cut into 4 pieces, ends trimmed

2 tablespoons Dijon mustard

2 tablespoons whole-grain mustard

1 cup wild arugula

1. Remove the grill grate from a charcoal grill and build a hot fire with lump charcoal until red-hot, raking the coals to spread out evenly.

2. Put on your fireproof gloves. Put the peppers and onion directly on top of the coals. The peppers will char pretty quickly, about 30 seconds to 1 minute per side; turn them often with tongs, until blackened on all sides. The onion will take longer, 10 to 12 minutes, until it is softened and dark at the edges.

3. Put the peppers in a medium stainless steel heatproof bowl, cover with plastic wrap, and let sweat for about 10 minutes to loosen the skins. Peel and rub off the charred skins. Split the peppers in half and remove the cores and seeds. Cut the peppers crosswise into thin strips and put into the same stainless steel bowl. Cut the onion in half from root to tip and peel off the charred skin. Slice the onion crosswise into thin strips and add to the bowl of peppers. Add the vinegar and olive oil and season with salt and 3 turns of a peppermill.

4. Lightly prick the sausages all over with a fork so that they do not burst while cooking. Put on your fireproof gloves again. Lay the sausages directly on top of the coals. Cook, turning periodically with tongs, for 8 to 10 minutes. Transfer the sausages to the bowl with the peppers and onion. Put the grill grate back on grill. Set the bowl on the coolest part of the grill to stay warm. Cut the rolls down the center lengthwise to open them up (but still hinged). Lay the rolls on the grill, cut-side down, and toast for 1 minute.

5. Combine the Dijon and whole-grain mustards in a small bowl. Spread 1 tablespoon of the mustard mixture on the bottom half of each roll; place 1 sausage and a handful of the arugula into each roll. Top with a good amount of the pepper-onion mixture and close the top half of the bread to make the sandwich.

WITH THE COALS

Setting out to open a restaurant where everything is cooked with live fire was challenging, not only from a permit perspective but also in terms of developing a uniquely varied menu for our guests to enjoy. Grilling, smoking, and burying food in the coals are surefire methods to achieve that smoky depth of flavor that only live fire can provide. However, for a subtle approach to delicate meat and fish, we began doing a coal-kissed cooking technique, where we take live embers from the fire and sear the protein directly with the coal. It allows us to honor the fundamental and inherent integrity of ingredients, yet deepen the flavor without adding too much to it.

On a recent trip to Tokyo, I was inspired and mesmerized watching a sushi chef take advantage of a flaming coal to quickly touch ocean-fresh unagi and salmon belly to singed perfection. Far better than a smelly butane torch, searing fish and meat with a live piece of coal cooks it slightly on just the thin outer layer, imparts a hint of sweet smokiness, and provides a different texture than you get from pure raw foods. The idea of using coals to kiss food to add the essence of wood smoke and char was so much fun that I took it and ran with it, and it is now a substantial part of our menu. Try it out with Ahi Tuna Tataki with Yuzu, Shiitake, and Radish (page 171); Scallop Carpaccio with Chimichurri and Lemon Bread Crumbs (page 173); and Singed New York Strip with Beef Fat Vinaigrette (page 181). You want to make sure you have an audience when you practice this coal-searing performance, as it's as enjoyable to cook as it is to watch. The key to success is to make sure the coals are large in size and bright red-hot, and be sure to have a baking sheet fitted with a wire rack insert and a couple of pairs of long metal tongs handy.

Adding activated charcoal is another way I like to achieve the nuance of smoky flavor without actually using a full-on fire. Found in powdered form at health food stores and online, food-safe activated charcoal is the by-product of burning a carbon source like wood or, more often, coconut shells. Frequently used to absorb toxins, this magic black powder lends a slightly smoky flavor and eye-catching pitch-black hue to recipes (Charcoal Flatbread, page 185, and Midnight Margarita, page 191). The ebony take on the classic cocktail is simply gorgeous and everybody goes nuts over it!

◇◇

Ahi Tuna Tataki with Yuzu, Shiitake, and Radish

SERVES 4

The Japanese dish tataki uses the process of quickly searing the outside of a piece of meat or fish, which leaves it rare in the center while creating a slight sear around the edges. While traditionally made in a hot skillet, for a better texture and flavor I like to "kiss" the tuna loin with a flaming hot coal to impart a distinctive, smoky flavor and subtle sear, and then thinly slice it. The Asian flavors of salty soy, sweet rice vinegar, and tart yuzu really show off the meaty qualities of tuna. Serve as a starter or light lunch.

2 tablespoons grapeseed oil

6 shiitake mushrooms, wiped of grit

Fine sea salt

2 teaspoons yuzu kosho paste (see Note)

1 tablespoon yuzu juice or lime juice

1 tablespoon soy sauce

1 tablespoon rice wine vinegar

¼ cup extra-virgin olive oil

1 plum (Roma) tomato, seeded and finely diced

2 scallions (green parts only), thinly sliced on a slight bias

One 8-ounce Ahi tuna loin, halved lengthwise

Fleur de sel

2 radishes, thinly sliced on a mandoline

1. Coat a wide sauté pan with grapeseed oil, heat over medium-low heat, and add the mushrooms; season lightly with salt. Sauté the mushrooms until they lose their moisture and begin to brown, 3 to 5 minutes. Transfer the mushrooms to a cutting board and finely dice. Set aside.

2. Wrap a damp towel around the base of a mixing bowl to hold it steady. Add the yuzu kosho paste, yuzu juice, soy sauce, vinegar, and 1 tablespoon water to the bowl. Mix with a small spoon or whisk until the yuzu kosho paste is smooth and fully incorporated into the liquids. Pour the olive oil in a slow, steady stream while whisking until the vinaigrette is emulsified. Add the reserved sautéed mushrooms, tomato, and scallions, stirring to incorporate. You should have about 1 cup. Set aside at room temperature to allow the flavors to come together while preparing the tuna.

3. Remove the grill grate from a charcoal grill and build a small, hot fire with lump charcoal until red-hot; the tuna is not actually cooked in the coals; instead, the burning coals are used to lightly sear the fish.

recipe continues

4. Put a wire rack on a rimmed baking sheet. Lay the tuna loin on the rack, top-side up. Using tongs, remove a large piece of glowing red-hot coal from the barbecue and set it on top of the tuna. Press the piece of coal on the surface of the tuna for a few seconds before moving it to another spot—the ultimate goal is to sear the side faceup with touches from the coals. The piece of coal begins to cool down in about 30 seconds, so keep repeating the process with new, fiery coals as you work on searing the entire surface of the tuna. The hotter the coal, the less likely it is to stick. If it does stick, it's not a big deal. Just carefully pull the tuna off the coal with another set of tongs.

5. Move the tuna loin to a cutting board and brush off the ash with a dry pastry brush. Thinly slice the tuna crosswise into planks. Shingle the tuna slices snug next to each other on a serving platter. Season lightly with fleur de sel. Spoon the yuzu vinaigrette around and over the tuna, and top with the slivered radishes.

Ingredient Note: Yuzu Kosho
Found primarily in Asian markets in a jar or tube, this fragrant spicy citrus paste hails from Japan and makes just about everything taste alive! I highly recommend seeking it out and incorporating it in your condiment arsenal. It's a secret weapon for adding an acidic-fiery kick and oomph to most Japanese-inspired dishes, or use it when you need a zesty accent to grilled meats, fish, vegetables, or even soups.

CHARCOAL

Scallop Carpaccio with Chimichurri and Lemon Bread Crumbs

SERVES 4

Impress guests with this simple and decadent starter or fish course, perfect for an al fresco dinner party. The scallops for this dish need to be spanking fresh so that the sweet, untainted flavor of the fish shines through. Thinly slicing the scallops, a la "carpaccio," and quickly searing one side using the coals gives you the best of both the raw and cooked worlds. The hint of ash truly activates the natural sweetness of the scallop while imparting a mild smoky flavor and melt-in-your-mouth texture. Scallops are tender and delicate and inclined to stick if the coals are not blazing hot, so be sure to use large pieces of fiery coal that retain the most heat. Chimichurri adds bright acidity to the tender scallop flesh, but for a simple alternative, drizzle with good olive oil, a spritz of lemon juice, and chopped fresh parsley.

4 large diver scallops (2 ounces each), muscle removed

Extra-virgin olive oil, for brushing

Fleur de sel

½ cup Smoked Paprika Chimichurri with Pickled Mustard Seeds (page 33)

¼ cup Lemon Bread Crumbs (page 77)

WITH THE COALS

1. Remove the grill grate from a charcoal grill and build a small, hot fire with lump charcoal until red-hot; the scallops are not actually cooked in the coals but, instead, you use the burning coals to lightly sear the scallops.

2. Put a wire rack on a rimmed baking sheet. Using a sharp knife, thinly slice each scallop crosswise into 4 to 5 discs and lay side by side on a platter. Lightly brush the surface of the scallops with olive oil. Using tongs, remove a large piece of glowing red-hot coal from the barbecue and set it on the wire rack. Gently lay a scallop slice, oil-side down, on top of the hot coal for 5 seconds—the flesh touching the coal will turn opaque and show bits of smoky ash on the surface. The piece of coal begins to cool down in about 30 seconds, so keep repeating the process with new, fiery coals as you work on searing all of the scallop slices. The hotter the coal, the less likely it is to stick. If it does stick, it's not a big deal. Just carefully pull the scallop off the coal with another set of tongs.

3. Brush off the ash with a dry pastry brush. Arrange the scallop slices, seared-sides up, snug next to each other on a serving platter. Season the seared scallops lightly with fleur de sel, spoon the chimichurri sauce around and over the scallops, and sprinkle with the bread crumbs.

Shrimp Scampi with Lemon, Parsley, and Garlic

SERVE 4

Pizza stones are remarkably versatile and good for more than just making homemade pizza. These ceramic squares and rounds stand up to high heat and hold it exceptionally well. You can make this dish outdoors tableside, so it's really cool to prepare in front of a crowd. Heat a pizza stone directly in the coals and then display it on top of bricks (for safety) on the dining table and cook the shrimp quickly right before everyone's eyes. I encourage you to try this cooking method with bay scallops and calamari rings as well, which also cook up in a flash. You can get a couple of bricks from a home improvement store and pizza stones are available online or at kitchen suppliers. Serve this dish as a hot appetizer.

2 tablespoons finely chopped fresh flat-leaf parsley, plus more for garnish

2 garlic cloves, minced after removing the germ (see Note, page 31)

Finely grated zest and juice of 1 lemon

1 teaspoon fine sea salt, plus more for seasoning

¼ teaspoon dried red pepper flakes

¼ cup extra-virgin olive oil, plus more for drizzling

12 extra jumbo (16/20) shrimp, peeled, deveined, and butterflied with tails on

Piment d'Espelette (see Note, page 34) or cayenne

1. Wrap two bricks in aluminum foil and lay them flat on the outdoor table you are serving on—the bricks will act as the stand for the pizza stone. Since you'll be setting the hot pizza stone to rest on top, be sure the bricks are about the same width as the stone.

2. Remove the grill grate from a charcoal grill and build a hot fire with lump charcoal until red-hot. Lay the pizza stone directly in the coals and heat for 20 to 30 minutes.

3. In a small mixing bowl, combine the parsley, garlic, lemon zest, lemon juice, 1 teaspoon salt, and red pepper flakes. Stir in ¼ cup olive oil until combined.

recipe continues

4. Put the shrimp in a medium mixing bowl, drizzle with olive oil, and season with salt and Piment d'Espelette. Toss to coat. Bring the shrimp and parsley oil to the table—and ask your guests to sit or stand around the table.

5. Using tongs, carefully carry the hot pizza stone to the table and set it on the bricks (this technique should be done only outdoors for safety). Lay the shrimp evenly on top of the hot pizza stone—they will begin to smoke and sizzle immediately. As the shrimp begin to become opaque and curl up, turn them over with tongs and press down gently with tongs to get a nice sear. Keep turning them to be sure all sides of the shrimp are cooked. The whole cooking process should take about 3 minutes. Spoon the parsley oil over the shrimp and turn them over again so they are well coated. Sprinkle with chopped parsley to garnish.

Eggs Black Benedict

SERVES 4

Decadence is what makes eggs Benedict a star of the brunch table; but black, velvety hollandaise makes this dish a visual showstopper. Even in my formative years, eggs Benedict was the go-to dish my sister and I would order when we visited our grandparents on weekends. So naturally, when I opened Charcoal and put together the brunch menu, the first dish that made the cut was this classic. Then, I thought, what could I do to reinvent a beloved, ubiquitous dish and make it unique to Charcoal restaurant? Smoky, jet-black charcoal hollandaise was the answer. There's an undeniable wow factor when you crack the bright yellow egg yolk into the black hollandaise, and you will find yourself making this showoff dish time after time. Just a heads-up, the charcoal hollandaise will likely leave a residual black outline on your, and your guests', lips—which thankfully isn't permanent.

8 slices country bread, about ½ inch thick

4 slices thick-cut smoked ham steak

Extra-virgin olive oil, for brushing

Hollandaise

2 large egg yolks, preferably organic and free-range

1 tablespoon activated charcoal powder (see Note, page 50)

Juice of ½ lemon

1 cup (2 sticks) unsalted butter, melted and warm

¼ teaspoon fine sea salt, plus more for seasoning

Pinch of cayenne

8 large eggs, preferably organic and free-range

1 tablespoon white vinegar

½ cup Charred Tomato Sauce (page 80)

Freshly ground black pepper

2 fresh chives, minced

1. Preheat a charcoal or gas grill to medium heat (350°F).

2. Brush both sides of the bread and ham slices with olive oil. Grill the ham steaks for 4 minutes per side and grill the bread for 1 minute per side. Remove from the grill. Cut the ham about the same size as the bread (you might have a little bit extra for snacking). Set aside.

3. Vigorously whisk the egg yolks, charcoal powder, 1 tablespoon of water, and the lemon juice together in a medium stainless steel bowl until slightly thickened. Set the bowl over a saucepan containing barely simmering water (the water should not touch the bottom of the bowl) and continue to whisk rapidly until the mixture is thick and doubled in volume. Be careful not to let the eggs get too hot, or they will scramble; move the bowl off the simmering water and continue to whisk if they look like they're cooking too fast.

recipe continues

4. Shut off the heat, remove the bowl, cover the pot of simmering water with a damp kitchen towel, and set the bowl back on top—the towel will hold the bowl steady as you whisk. Slowly drizzle in the melted butter and continue to whisk over the water until the sauce is thickened and doubled in volume. Remove from the heat and whisk in the salt and cayenne. Cover and place in a warm spot until ready to use for the eggs Benedict. If the sauce gets too thick, whisk in a few drops of warm water before serving.

5. Fill a wide saucepan halfway with water, add the vinegar, and bring to a simmer over medium heat. When the water is just barely bubbling, carefully crack 1 egg on a flat surface—not on the lip of a bowl—into a small cup or ladle. Gently pour the egg into the simmering water with one continuously slow tilt. Repeat with the remaining eggs—you can easily poach 2 or 3 eggs at a time, spacing them apart in the pot. Poach the eggs just until the whites are set but the yolks are still soft, about 3 minutes. Use a slotted spoon to transfer the eggs to a plate. Dab the bottom of the eggs with paper towels to blot dry.

6. To assemble, put 2 slices of bread on the base of each plate and spread each with 1 tablespoon of the tomato sauce. Place a slice of grilled ham on top, followed by a poached egg. Season with salt and a couple of turns of a peppermill. Spoon the hollandaise sauce over the eggs. Garnish with the minced chives.

Singed New York Strip with Beef Fat Vinaigrette

SERVES 4

Inspired by the plethora of Korean barbecue houses we are lucky to have in L.A., here, thinly sliced steak is briefly laid over a hot coal to sear just until singed and smoky on the outside, and rare and tender on the inside. This unique way of cooking always gets everyone's attention!

1 boneless dry-aged prime New York strip steak (12 to 14 ounces), about 1½ inches thick

Extra-virgin olive oil, for brushing

Fleur de sel

½ cup Beef Fat Vinaigrette (recipe follows), at room temperature

Freshly ground black pepper

2 fresh chives, finely chopped

2 ounces Parmesan cheese, shaved with a vegetable peeler

1. Remove the grill grate from a charcoal grill and build a small, hot fire with lump charcoal until red-hot. The steak is not actually cooked in the coals; the burning coals are used to lightly sear the meat.

2. Put a wire rack on a rimmed baking sheet. Thinly slice the steak crosswise into about twenty-five ¼-ounce pieces and lay side by side on a platter—discard the tail end of the steak, called the chain, as it is too sinewy for this cooking method. Lightly brush the surface of the steak with olive oil. Using tongs, remove a large piece of glowing red-hot coal from the barbecue and set it on the wire rack. Gently lay the steak, oil-side down, on top of the hot coal for 5 seconds. The flesh touching the coal will change color and show bits of smoky ash on the surface. Note that the piece of coal begins to cool down in about 30 seconds, so keep repeating the process with new, fiery coals as you work on searing all of the meat slices. The hotter the coal, the less likely it is to stick. If it does stick, it's not a big deal. Just carefully pull the steak off the coal with another set of tongs.

3. Brush off the ash with a dry pastry brush. Arrange the seared beef slices on a serving platter, season with fleur de sel, drizzle the vinaigrette around and over the steak, and top with 6 turns of a peppermill, the chopped chives, and shaved Parmesan.

recipe continues

Beef Fat Vinaigrette

MAKES ¾ CUP

Unlike oil, beef fat adds next-level flavor to vinaigrette, making for a meatier, richer experience. The thick, viscous dressing is a natural for steak but also adds a nuanced beef flavor to sturdy greens, such as escarole or Swiss chard. You can buy scrap beef fat from your butcher pretty inexpensively. If you have leftover vinaigrette, before using be sure to heat or bring to room temperature if congealed.

¼ pound beef fat, cut into small chunks

1½ teaspoons Dijon mustard

1 small garlic clove, smashed into a paste after removing the germ (see Note, page 31)

½ small shallot, minced

¼ cup sherry vinegar or Basque Vinegar (page 34)

½ teaspoon fine sea salt

Freshly ground black pepper

¼ cup grapeseed oil

1 tablespoon extra-virgin olive oil

Juice of ¼ lemon

3 fresh chives, finely chopped

1. Put the beef fat in a small saucepan and cover with ½ cup water. Heat over medium-low heat. Gently simmer until the fat melts and renders out completely and the water evaporates, 15 to 20 minutes. Strain the beef fat through a fine-mesh strainer into a glass measuring cup and discard the bits of leftover beef. You should end up with a little more than ¼ cup of beef fat. Set aside.

2. In a jar or container with a tight-fitting lid, combine the mustard, garlic, shallot, vinegar, 1 tablespoon water, salt, and 6 turns of a peppermill. Shake well. Add the grapeseed oil, olive oil, and rendered beef fat. Shake well again to combine. Add the lemon juice and chives and shake again to incorporate. The vinaigrette may be stored, covered, in the refrigerator for up to 1 month. Thaw and gently reheat on the stove or in the microwave before using, as the fats will rise to the top and separate when refrigerated. Once heated, whisk well to incorporate the oils.

Charcoal Flatbread

MAKES TEN FLATBREADS

My chef de cuisine at Charcoal, Joe Johnson, developed this recipe to accompany our signature beef tartare appetizer (Beef Tartare with Seeds and Spices, page 234). Better than toast points, the sour undertones from the buttermilk and the activated powdered charcoal transform the bread into a jet-black crust of deliciousness. Serve the flatbread with Kabocha Squash Hummus (page 134) for dipping and Grilled Lamb Chops with Charred Eggplant Puree (page 121) for wrapping. Flatbread is an ultimate canvas for creativity, perfect to adorn with a rotating crop of vibrant, seasonal ingredients that fall outside the bounds of the traditional pizzeria, although this quick flatbread also makes a stunning Margherita pizza topped with tomato sauce, cheese, and basil. You will have plenty of dough from this master recipe to freeze and use at whim.

2 teaspoons active dry yeast

Pinch of sugar

1½ cups buttermilk

5 cups all-purpose flour, plus more for dusting

2 tablespoons activated charcoal powder (see Note, page 50)

¼ cup extra-virgin olive oil, plus more for brushing the dough

3 teaspoons fine sea salt

Vegetable oil, for greasing the grill

1. In the bowl of a standing electric mixer fitted with a dough hook, combine the yeast, sugar, and ½ cup warm water. Stir gently to dissolve. Let the mixture stand until the yeast comes alive and starts to foam, 5 to 7 minutes.

2. Turn the mixer on low and gradually pour in the buttermilk. Slowly add the flour in three batches, adding the charcoal powder in the last batch. When the dough starts to come together, increase the speed to medium and add the olive oil and salt. Stop the machine periodically to scrape the dough off the hook. Knead the dough in the mixer until the dough is a beautiful dark gray mass and is no longer sticky, about 10 minutes.

3. Turn the dough onto a lightly floured work surface and knead for a few minutes with floured hands. Knead by folding the dough over itself and pushing out with the heel of your hands, not down. Rotate the dough a quarter turn and repeat. Continue until you have rotated and kneaded the dough all the way around. The dough is properly kneaded when

recipe continues

you can stretch it without breaking and, when you press on the dough with your fingertips, it springs back quickly.

4. Form the dough into a round and place in a large mixing bowl, cover with plastic wrap or a damp towel, and let it rise in a warm place until doubled in size, about 30 minutes. Test the dough by pressing 2 fingers into it. If indents remain, the dough is adequately risen.

5. Divide the dough into ten 4-ounce balls and set on a baking sheet or platter. Allow to rest for 10 minutes so the dough has a second rise (this will help make it light and crispy when it bakes).

6. If you are not going to bake all of the balls, lightly coat a few pieces of plastic wrap with nonstick cooking spray and use them to tightly wrap the dough individually. The flatbread dough will keep in the refrigerator for up to 5 days or frozen for up to 3 months. Defrost overnight in the refrigerator before rolling and grilling.

7. If you are grilling the flatbread immediately, preheat a charcoal or gas grill to medium-high heat (400 to 450°F).

8. Take a few paper towels and fold them several times to make a thick square. Blot a small amount of vegetable oil on the paper towel, then carefully and quickly wipe the hot grates of the grill. This will create a nonstick grilling surface.

9. On a lightly floured surface and with a floured rolling pin, roll each ball of dough into a rustic round shape. It doesn't need to be perfect circle but should be about ¼ inch thick.

10. Lightly brush the dough with olive oil to create a sheen on the surface of the crust. Using tongs, put the flatbread, oil-side down, on the grill and cook for 1½ to 2 minutes. Brush the surface with vegetable oil, flip the dough over, and grill the other side for an additional 1½ to 2 minutes.

11. Using tongs, put the flatbread on a cutting board and cut it into wedges with a sharp knife or pizza cutter, if desired. Serve warm.

Lemon Meringue Tarts

SERVES 6

I'm not a big dessert person, but when I indulge, I crave fruit-centric sweets instead of chocolate. These little individual lemon tarts showcase the zingy pucker and intoxicating fragrance of my favorite citrus; if you can get your hands on Meyer lemons, definitely use them in the curd for a sweeter, fuller flavor. This classic lemon meringue recipe has been part of my repertoire for years, prepared the traditional way. For the final fiery touch, I use hot coal to caramelize the meringue instead of a standard kitchen torch, giving the meringue a s'mores-like gooeyness. As with most baking, there are a few elements to this dessert, but thankfully all can be prepared ahead of time. You will need six 4-inch-round individual tart/quiche pans with removable bottoms to bake them in, which are available online or at kitchen stores.

Pastry

1 pound (4 sticks) unsalted butter, at room temperature, cut into chunks

1 cup sugar

1 large egg, preferably organic and free-range

1 teaspoon pure vanilla extract

Pinch of fine sea salt

4 cups all-purpose flour, sifted

Lemon Curd

3 large egg yolks, preferably organic and free-range

1 large egg, preferably organic and free-range

¾ cup sugar

Finely grated zest and juice of 3 lemons, preferably Meyer

4 tablespoons (½ stick) unsalted butter, cold and cut into small cubes

Meringue

3 large egg whites, preferably organic and free-range, at room temperature

½ teaspoon freshly squeezed lemon juice

¾ cup caster (superfine) sugar

Pinch of fine sea salt

¼ teaspoon pure vanilla extract

1. Make the pastry: Put the butter and sugar in the bowl of a standing electric mixer fitted with a paddle attachment, or use a handheld electric mixer. Beat on medium speed until light and fluffy, about 3 minutes. Scrape down the sides of the bowl with a rubber spatula. Add the egg, vanilla, and salt and mix on low speed until fully incorporated. Scrape down the sides of the bowl with the spatula. Gradually add the flour in 3 batches, beating well to combine and scraping the sides of the bowl after each addition. Form the dough into a disk, wrap in plastic, and refrigerate for at least 1 hour or up to 2 days to firm it up.

2. Make the lemon curd: In a small saucepan, whisk together the egg yolks and whole egg until combined. Slowly sprinkle in the sugar while continuing to whisk. Whisk until creamy and well incorporated. Place the pot over medium heat and add the lemon zest and lemon juice. Whisk constantly until the custard is thick and yellow and can coat the back of a spoon, 8 to 10 minutes (don't let it boil). Remove from the heat and whisk in the cold

recipe continues

butter, 1 piece at a time, until melted. Strain the lemon curd through a fine-mesh sieve to remove any pulp and make the custard smooth. Cover with a piece of plastic wrap directly on the surface to prevent a skin from forming, and refrigerate for at least 1 hour or up to 2 days. The curd will thicken further as it chills.

3. Assemble the tarts: Remove the pastry from the refrigerator. Roll it out on a lightly floured surface to a 12-inch rectangle of about ⅛ inch thickness with a floured rolling pin. Cut the pastry into six squares and fit into each 4-inch tart pan with removable bottoms. Roll any scraps and leftover dough into a disc, wrap in plastic, and reserve for another use. With your fingertips, press evenly into the sides of the ring, especially the scalloped edges. Trim off any excess hanging dough. Chill for at least 30 minutes.

4. Preheat the oven to 350°F.

5. Prick the bottom of each piece of pastry with the tines of a fork. Line the shells carefully with aluminum foil, pressing well into the edges so the pastry does not shrink while baking. Fill with weights, uncooked rice, or dry beans, making sure you get all the way into the edges to prevent shrinkage.

6. Place the tart pans on a rimmed baking sheet (this will make it easier to move them in and out of the oven) and bake just until the pastry begins to brown around the edges, 10 to 12 minutes. Carefully remove the foil and weights and continue baking until evenly light brown, about 5 more minutes. Watch the pastry carefully, as ovens vary and pastry can brown very quickly. Cool completely for at least 15 minutes before filling with the curd. Fill each shell with about ½ cup of lemon curd and spread evenly to the edges with a small offset spatula. Remove the tarts from the molds and set aside.

7. Make the meringue: Combine the egg whites and lemon juice in the bowl of a standing electric mixer fitted with a wire whisk attachment, or use a handheld electric mixer. Beat on medium-low speed until the egg whites are foamy. Increase the speed to medium and beat until soft peaks form, about 2 minutes. With the mixer running, gradually pour in the sugar in a thin stream over the fluffed egg whites. Beat until the egg whites are stiff and glossy, about 4 minutes. Remove the bowl from the mixer and fold in the salt and vanilla.

8. Transfer the meringue to a pastry bag fitted with a ½-inch plain tip and pipe the meringue 2 inches high onto each tart, completely covering the lemon curd.

9. Remove the grill grate from a charcoal grill and build a small, hot fire with lump charcoal until red-hot; the hot coals will be used to torch the meringue.

10. Using tongs, remove a large piece of glowing red-hot coal from the barbecue and set it on top of the meringue. Press the piece of coal on the surface for several seconds before moving it to another spot—the ultimate goal is to "torch" the meringue with the coals. The piece of coal begins to cool down in about 30 seconds, so keep repeating the process with new, fiery coals as you work on searing each tart.

11. The lemon meringue tarts are best the same day they are assembled. They can be refrigerated for 4 to 6 hours. Remove them from the refrigerator 20 minutes before serving.

Midnight Margarita

SERVES 6

A stone's throw from the Pacific Ocean, the bar at Charcoal draws a lively, local crowd and often gets hopping before the sun sets over Venice Beach. Seductive-looking and equally delicious, our signature black margarita is a reimagined adaptation of the beloved classic, with tart lime foam, black smoked salt, and charcoal-infused tequila tinted jet-black from my restaurant's namesake ingredient. Trust me, your guests will be talking about it for days! Credit for this creative cocktail goes to master mixologist Pablo Moix, who consulted on our bar program and developed our most famous drink.

12 ounces silver tequila

1 teaspoon activated charcoal powder (see Note, page 50)

½ cup freshly squeezed lime juice

1 tablespoon lecithin (see Note)

2 teaspoons finely ground smoked sea salt

For Each Margarita

Finely ground smoked sea salt, for rimming the glass

1 lime wedge, plus more for serving

1 large ice cube or sphere

2 ounces (¼ cup) charcoal-infused tequila

1 ounce (2 tablespoons) freshly squeezed lime juice

½ ounce (1 tablespoon) Cointreau orange liqueur

½ ounce (1 tablespoon) agave nectar

1. In a liquid measuring cup or empty bottle, mix the tequila with the charcoal powder until black.

2. To prepare the froth, combine 1 cup water, the lime juice, lecithin, and smoked sea salt in a container with high sides. Just before you are ready to serve the cocktail, whisk vigorously with a small whisk (or use a frothing wand if you have one), until the lime water is thick and frothy. Froth each time before using.

3. Sprinkle a saucer or small plate with smoked sea salt to cover the bottom. Use a lime wedge to moisten the rim of an old-fashioned glass, turn the glass upside down, and firmly dip into the smoked sea salt so it sticks. Turn the glass upright and add the large ice cube.

4. For each margarita, combine 2 ounces of the charcoal tequila with 1 ounce of lime juice, ½ ounce Cointreau, and ½ ounce of agave in a shaker with regular ice cubes; shake it up really well until the tin looks misty on the outside. Strain the Margarita into the glass. Rake off the foamy surface of the lime froth with a tablespoon and spoon on top of the Margarita. Garnish with a lime wedge.

Ingredient Note: Lecithin

Derived from soybeans, lecithin is widely sold as a nutritional supplement due to its potential health benefits. From a food standpoint, soy lecithin is a terrific emulsifier and is the magic powder that stabilizes the margarita foam, keeping it aerated with tiny bubbles for several minutes. It's possible to still froth the liquid without the lecithin, but the foam won't hold as long. Lecithin is available in powder, liquid, or pellet-like granules, and all will work in this recipe.

WITH THE SMOKE

I have massive respect for the professional pit-masters who dedicate their lives to the cooking and culture of competition barbecue. Whether smoking a whole hog, racks of ribs, or hunks of brisket, the traditional barbecue regions of North Carolina, Texas, and Kansas City take smoking very, very seriously. People spend years refining their craft in the barbecue pro circuit, harnessing the science of fire, smoke, and food into a genuine sport. With that said, I am not a barbecue expert. There are plenty of great books dedicated to the art of long smoking. My goal in this chapter is to speak to the back-yard barbecue enthusiast and keep the smoking process fairly simple, while still enjoying the remarkable flavor that cooking with wood produces. While you certainly can use a fancy (and expensive) offset barrel smoker or vertical water smoker to prepare these recipes, all can be made using a Kamado ceramic grill (e.g., Big Green Egg) or kettle grill (e.g., Weber), one of which you likely already own.

A few years ago, my kids gifted me a Big Green Egg for Father's Day, and after I grilled just about everything under the sun, I delved into using it for smoking. Smoke adds a rich deep flavor not only to meat, but also to a host of ingredients such as vegetables, fish, and even ice. The majority of dishes smoke for a relatively short time using a technique I like to call "grill smoking," which relies on direct heat. Adding wood chips or chunks to hot charcoal, closing the lid, and working the vents allow your grill to maintain a lower temperature and also keeps the smoke contained inside to infuse flavor into your food.

◇◇

GRILL-SMOKING PROCESS

To set up either a ceramic grill or kettle grill for grill smoking:

Fill the grill halfway with lump charcoal and open the bottom vent all of the way to get air to the coals. Light the coals with fire starters (or you may light the coals in a chimney starter and carefully add to the grill). Once the majority of the coals are lit, close the lid and adjust the vents to reach the temperature indicated in the recipe (open to raise the heat; close to reduce the heat). Now, add unsoaked wood chips or chunks as specified in the recipe (I find soaking the wood an unnecessary step and often the chips/chunks smolder too much, leaving a bitter aftertaste to whatever I'm smoking). It's important not to add the wood until you reach the correct smoking temperature and you are ready to cook so you don't waste the smoke. Set the grill grate in place, add the food to the grill, and close the lid immediately. Adjust the vents as needed during cooking to maintain the appropriate temperature.

The only dishes that are long smoked using low, indirect heat are Herb-Brined Smoked Turkey (page 208), Smoked Lamb Ribs with Fermented Black Beans and Charred Scallion Vinaigrette (page 205), and Smoked and Grilled Bone-In Short Ribs with Barbecue Sauce (page 217). By all means, if you have a traditional smoker, use it for these recipes. You will still be able to achieve successful results with a Kamado ceramic grill (i.e., Big Green Egg), but truthfully, it will be a little bit more challenging using a kettle grill (i.e., Weber), as you'll need to be more attentive and add coals during the cook. The longest smoke is six hours for the short ribs, which in the scheme of true smoked barbecue isn't even that long.

CERAMIC GRILL SMOKING

To use a ceramic grill for smoking, you will need to purchase a heat deflector, such as the Big Green Egg's convEGGtor, to create the indirect cooking environment required for smoking. Also called a plate setter, this adds a barrier between the food and the direct heat of the fire but also allows the hot air and smoke to circulate around the food.

Fill the fire chamber with lump charcoal and scatter the unsoaked wood chips or chunks on top of the coals as specified in the recipe. Open the bottom vent all of the way to get air to the coals. Light the coals with fire starters (or you may light the coals in a chimney starter and carefully add them to the grill). Once a few of the coals have ignited, carefully insert the plate setter on top. Set a disposable aluminum pan filled halfway with water or apple juice on top of the plate. Place the cooking grate on top. Close the lid and adjust the vents to reach the temperature indicated in the recipe (open to raise the heat; close to reduce the heat). Keep a close eye on the size of the fire as it warms up so that the smoker doesn't get too hot, as it's much harder to cool the fire down in a ceramic grill than it is to bump it up a few degrees. Once the temperature is reached, add the food and close the lid immediately. Adjust the vents as needed during cooking to maintain the appropriate temperature. Even for the six-hour smoke, you should not have to worry about adding more coals as the ceramic grill is well insulated and holds heat extremely well. When you are done smoking, close the lid and the vents to extinguish the coals.

KETTLE GRILL SMOKING

Set up your kettle grill by creating a two-zone barbecue setup, which provides smoke and an indirect heat source. Bank a pile of unlit charcoal against one side of the grill, filling up halfway, and light with fire starters (or you may light the coals in a chimney starter and carefully add to one side of the grill). This is your hot zone. Make sure your vents on the bottom of the grill are open and not clogged with ash. Put a disposable aluminum pan filled halfway with water or apple juice on the empty side of the grill. This is your cool zone. Set the grill grate in place. Position the grate with a handle over the coals—this makes adding more coal easier later on (some models have hinged grates for this purpose). Close the lid and adjust the vents to reach the temperature indicated in the recipe (open to raise the heat; close to reduce the heat). Place the meat on the grill grate on the cool zone side above the water pan. Place the lid on so the vent holes are positioned over the meat and leave them open at least halfway so the smoke will be drawn up and over the meat to escape.

The smoke time for the lamb ribs, turkey, and short ribs ranges from three to six hours, so it is highly likely that you will need to add more coals to your kettle grill, as it burns more quickly and is not as insulated as a ceramic grill. As the fire burns down, add more unlit coals on top of the lit ones in the grill with a small shovel. Take care to always wear fireproof gloves.

A WORD ON WOOD

There are a wide range of woods that can impart smoky flavor and complexity, from mild and sweet to strong and musky. The type of wood will have an impact on the finished taste of the food. But beware: It is easy to ruin food with too much wood. I'm a fan of applewood, maplewood, and cherrywood for smoking as they emit a fragrant, floral smoke for a balanced fruity flavor. It's best to use chunks instead of chips; they burn longer and I find that chips give off an unpleasant sawdust essence to food. I use stronger-flavored mesquite wood for the Old-Fashioned with Smoked Ice (page 221), as the sagebrush flavor is the ultimate match for the smokiness of bourbon. Wood chunks (and chips if you must) are available in bags at big box home improvement stores, barbecue stores, and even some grocery stores, especially in the summer.

Smoked Fingerling Potatoes with Cipollini Onions

SERVES 4 TO 6

Potatoes and onions are a classic combination that never goes out of style. To make this all-purpose side dish, you just need to give the vegetable a quick smoke, so you don't need a fancy smoker. Simply add a small amount of wood chips or a couple of chunks to your charcoal grill and that will do the trick. Pronounced chip-oh-LEE-nee, cipollini are flattened flying saucer–shaped onions from Italy that have a distinctly sweet flavor and crisp texture. The good news is that they are becoming widely available in markets. If you can't locate them, substitute pearl onions or shallots.

18 large fingerling potatoes (about 1½ pounds)

2 tablespoons kosher salt, plus more for grilling

2 garlic cloves

2 fresh thyme sprigs

1 tablespoon whole black peppercorns

10 cipollini onions, peeled

Extra-virgin olive oil

2 teaspoons sumac

Herb Vinaigrette (recipe follows)

Fleur de sel

Special Equipment

2 applewood or maplewood chunks or chips, or 1 large handful (about ½ cup), and a vegetable grill basket

1. Put the potatoes, salt, garlic, thyme, and peppercorns in a large saucepan. Fill with cold water to cover the potatoes. Bring to a boil over medium-high heat and cook until the potatoes are fork-tender, 20 to 25 minutes. Drain and set aside until cool enough to handle. While still warm, peel off the skin of the potatoes with your fingers. Cut the potatoes into ½-inch-thick rounds.

2. While the potatoes are boiling, prepare and preheat your grill to 250°F, following the grill-smoking method on page 194. Distribute the wood chunks or chips evenly around the coals and close the lid. Adjust the vents to maintain 250°F.

3. Place the potato slices in a grill basket. Toss the onions lightly with olive oil, salt, and sumac. Place the basket of potatoes on the grill and put the onions directly on the rack. Close the lid. Smoke for 20 minutes. Remove the potatoes from the grill and cover to keep warm. Open up the vents to increase the temperature to 300 to 350°F. Close the lid and continue to cook the onions for another 10 minutes.

4. Cut the onions into quarters and transfer to a serving bowl. Add the potatoes and toss with the vinaigrette. Season with fleur de sel and serve warm.

Herb Vinaigrette

MAKES ABOUT ½ CUP

My grandmother used to make a dressing similar to this that she would put on her potato salad. Fresh and light, this all-purpose vinaigrette is tangy and aromatic.

2 teaspoons Dijon mustard

2 tablespoons Champagne vinegar

1 tablespoon finely chopped fresh flat-leaf parsley leaves

1 tablespoon chopped chervil (optional)

1 teaspoon finely chopped fresh tarragon

½ shallot, minced

Finely grated zest of 1 lemon

¼ teaspoon fine sea salt

3 tablespoons grapeseed oil

1 tablespoon extra-virgin olive oil

Freshly ground black pepper

In a jar or container with a tight-fitting lid, combine the mustard, vinegar, parsley, chervil (if using), tarragon, shallot, lemon zest, salt, and 1 teaspoon water. Secure the lid and shake well. Add the grapeseed oil, olive oil, and 3 turns of a peppermill. Shake well again. The vinaigrette may be stored, covered, in the refrigerator for up to 3 months.

Smoked Mushroom and Beet Tartare with Currants

SERVES 4

When I launched Charcoal, I wanted to be sure it was not solely a carnivore's restaurant and featured vegetarian options that celebrated the fresh produce that California is famous for. While a section of our menu is dedicated to meat tartare—beef, venison, and lamb—I felt it equally important to showcase a vegetable-forward incarnation that shines with the seasons' finest. Executed on a grill-smoker, meaty mushrooms are the star of this colorful appetizer and soak up the smoke beautifully. The layers of colors and textures contrast one another well with crunchiness from the candied walnuts, chewiness from the mushrooms and currants, and creaminess from the crème fraîche, all balanced by the brightness of fresh herbs and lemon zest. The characteristic earthiness of raw beets—or as some say, "dirt taste"—is mellowed after briefly soaking in vinegar and salt.

Special Equipment

3 applewood chunks or 3 large handfuls (about 1½ cups) chips, and a vegetable grill basket

2 large portobello mushroom caps, wiped of grit

12 large white mushrooms, stemmed, wiped of grit, and quartered

Fine sea salt

1 large red beet, washed, peeled, and coarsely grated on a box grater

2 tablespoons sherry vinegar

1 cup crème fraîche

Finely grated zest of 1 lemon

2 tablespoons candied walnuts, coarsely chopped

2 tablespoons dried currants

2 tablespoons non-pareil capers, drained

½ shallot, finely minced

20 fresh flat-leaf parsley leaves, finely chopped

4 fresh chives, finely chopped

1 tablespoon extra-virgin olive oil

1 tablespoon walnut oil

Freshly ground black pepper

Charcoal Flatbread (page 185) or grilled or toasted sliced baguette, for serving

1. Prepare and preheat the grill to 325°F, following the grill-smoking method on page 194. Distribute the wood chunks or chips evenly around the coals and close the lid. Adjust the vents to maintain 325°F.

2. Put the portobello mushrooms and white mushrooms in a grill basket and season lightly with salt. Put the grill basket of mushrooms on the rack and close the lid. Smoke for 15 to 20 minutes, until the mushrooms have shrunk a bit and are tender. Remove the mushrooms from the grill, lightly season again, and set aside to cool. Grind the mushrooms through a meat grinder attachment fitted with a coarse plate. If you don't have one, you can pulse it in the bowl of a food processor or coarsely chop the mushrooms with a knife.

recipe continues

3. In a small mixing bowl, combine the grated beets with 1 tablespoon of vinegar and a pinch of salt. Toss and set aside for 5 to 10 minutes. In a separate small bowl, combine the crème fraîche and lemon zest.

4. In a medium mixing bowl, combine the mushrooms, walnuts, currants, capers, shallot, parsley, and chives. Add the remaining 1 tablespoon vinegar, the olive oil, and walnut oil. Season to taste with salt and 10 turns of a peppermill. Toss to combine. Strain the beets for a couple of minutes to make sure all of the liquid is removed. Put the grated beets into the bottom of a 2-cup glass bowl, pressing down with the back of a spoon to make an even layer. Top with the mushroom mixture, pressing down to make sure it is smooth, and then spread the crème fraîche mixture on top. Cover and refrigerate for 1 hour. Let your guests serve themselves and spoon the tartare onto individual plates. Serve with flatbread.

Smoked Cauliflower with Curry and Dates

SERVES 4 TO 6

This crowd-pleasing vegetable dip is a relatively quick affair using your charcoal grill and some added wood chips or chunks. An exotic mix of sweet, savory, and spicy, ras el hanout is a fragrant Moroccan spice blend that is akin to Indian curry (which may be substituted), and it makes notoriously bland cauliflower intriguing. Smoking the cauliflower gives it a meaty flavor and golden-charred color. The vibrant spinach dip is downright addictive and works well with raw crudités as well.

Special Equipment

2 applewood or maplewood chunks or 1 large handful (about ½ cup) chips

1 head cauliflower (about 2 pounds), with greens and stem intact

Extra-virgin olive oil

Fine sea salt

2 tablespoons ras el hanout

Grapeseed oil

1 small sweet onion, diced

8 Medjool dates, pitted and chopped

2 cups baby spinach

1 cup fresh cilantro leaves

¼ cup maple syrup

2 tablespoons Champagne vinegar

½ cup plus 1 generous tablespoon plain whole-milk Greek yogurt

¼ cup toasted almonds, coarsely chopped

Fleur de sel

1. Prepare and preheat the grill to 300°F, following the grill-smoking method on page 194. Distribute the wood chunks or chips evenly around the coals and close the lid. Adjust the vents to maintain 300°F.

2. Drizzle the cauliflower with olive oil and season with salt. Put the cauliflower on the rack and close the lid. Smoke for about 1½ hours. The cauliflower should be tender. Check by piercing with a cake tester or paring knife. If not tender, continue smoking for 10 minutes more.

3. Heat a dry sauté pan over low heat. Add the ras el hanout and toast for just a minute to release the fragrant oils, shaking the pan periodically to prevent scorching.

4. Place a large sauté pan over medium heat and coat with about ⅛ inch of grapeseed oil. Add the onion and cook, stirring, until soft and translucent, about 5 minutes. Add the dates and toasted ras el hanout and mix well to combine with the onions. Add the spinach and cilantro and season lightly with salt. After the spinach is wilted, about 2 minutes, stir in the maple syrup and vinegar. Cook for 1 minute, until the spinach is glazed. Remove the pan from the heat and mix in ½ cup of the yogurt until well combined. Put the remaining 1 tablespoon yogurt in a blender and add 1 tablespoon water—this will help the blades turn while pureeing the spinach mixture. Transfer the spinach mixture to the blender and puree until smooth. You should end up with about 2 cups. Spoon the dip into a serving bowl and fold in the almonds.

5. Cut the cauliflower through the core into 6 wedges and arrange on a serving platter around the dip. Sprinkle the cauliflower with fleur de sel and a drizzle of olive oil.

Cedar Plank Salmon with Hibiscus

SERVES 4 TO 6

It's easy to make perfectly smoked salmon just with your grill—all you need are some wood chunks/chips, a cedar plank, and a charcoal fire ready to go. Smoking doesn't have to take hours, especially for oily fish like salmon, which absorbs the smoky vapors readily. The low heat guarantees the salmon will be perfectly pink in the center and not dried out. You also need to be sure to take the salmon off the grill to rest periodically. If you grill often, you likely are familiar with cedar planks, which impart a woodsy, robust flavor to salmon and solve the problem of the fish falling apart and through the grates. You can pick up cedar planks in grilling and kitchen stores, or order them online. Be sure to soak the plank in water to prevent it from burning on the grill. In this dish, the floral essence of the hibiscus rub counterbalances the fatty richness of salmon. Serve with Grilled Asparagus with Chopped Egg Vinaigrette (page 73) or a simple butter lettuce salad.

1½ to 2 pounds skinless center-cut salmon fillet, preferably wild, pin bones removed

¼ cup Hibiscus Flower Rub (page 43)

10 fresh thyme sprigs

Special Equipment

3 applewood or cherrywood chunks or 4 large handfuls (about 2 cups) chips, and 1 cedar grilling plank

I. Lay the salmon in a medium baking dish and sprinkle the top with the hibiscus flower rub. Refrigerate, uncovered, for 2 to 4 hours. Take the fish out of the refrigerator about 30 minutes before cooking so it can come up to room temperature.

2. Fill a bowl with cool water and toss in the thyme for added flavor and fragrance. Put the cedar plank in the water, weighing it down with a heavy can or skillet to keep it submerged. Soak for 1 hour; this will help preserve the cedar plank because the water saturation will make it less likely to burn and will also impart moisture to keep the salmon from drying out.

3. Prepare and preheat the grill to 250 to 300°F, following the grill-smoking method on page 194. Distribute one-third of the wood chips or 1 chunk evenly in the coals and close the lid. Adjust the vents to maintain 250 to 300°F. Remove the cedar plank from the water and lay the salmon on top, rub-side up.

recipe continues

4. Place the plank with the salmon on the grill grate. Close the lid and let smoke for 5 minutes. Transfer the plank with salmon to a side table to rest for 3 minutes; be sure to close the grill lid to maintain the temperature and smoke. Open the lid, sprinkle in another third of the wood chips or 1 more chunk, and put the plank with salmon back on the grill. Close the lid and smoke for another 5 minutes. Remove the plank with salmon again to rest for 3 minutes. Add the final batch of wood chips or last chunk and return the salmon to the grill for 4 minutes. Repeat the resting and smoking process one last time (not adding chips/chunk in the final stage) for 4 minutes. The smoking process takes about 18 minutes, plus resting stages in between. The salmon should be between medium-rare and medium and pink in the center.

5. Allow the salmon to rest for 5 minutes before cutting. Serve the smoked salmon directly on the cedar plank.

Smoked Lamb Ribs with Fermented Black Beans and Charred Scallion Vinaigrette

SERVES 4 TO 6

Since we eat baby back pork ribs and beef ribs, why not change it up with lamb? With a layer of meat that's tender and flavorful, lamb ribs are relatively inexpensive and make for such good eating right off the bone. Sleek Denver-cut ribs are just lamb ribs that include seven or so bones from the breast, much like spareribs (also known as St. Louis–style). The Fermented Black Bean Rub (page 46) imparts an edgy flavor that tames the gaminess of the lamb. Serve with Smoked Cauliflower with Curry and Dates (page 201).

1 batch Fermented Black Bean Rub (page 46)

1 cup Red Wine Chipotle Barbecue Sauce (page 35), plus more for serving

3 racks of lamb (1½ pounds each), Denver-cut

Charred Scallion Vinaigrette (recipe follows)

Special Equipment

3 applewood chunks

1. Mix 2 tablespoons of the fermented black bean rub with the barbecue sauce and set aside. Dust each lamb rack with the remaining fermented black bean rub; make sure each rack is coated evenly and completely. Set aside at room temperature.

2. Prepare and preheat the smoker to 220°F as directed on page 194. Distribute the wood chunks around the coals and close the lid. Adjust the vents to maintain 220°F.

3. Place the lamb on the rack, making sure there is ample space between each piece. Close the lid.

4. The temperature of the smoker needs to be around 220°F. This is done by controlling the vents to restrict the flow of oxygen. Make small adjustments—open the vent more to raise the temperature and close to reduce it.

recipe continues

5. After 2½ hours, brush the sauce on the ribs to coat. At this point you may need to replenish the coals, if necessary. Close the lid and continue to smoke for an additional 30 minutes. Start checking the lamb for doneness; the internal temperature should be between 190 and 200°F. A great way to visually tell if the ribs are done is by picking the lamb up with tongs by the center of the rack—if the ends sag down, the ribs are done. If not, return the ribs to the smoker and check every

30 minutes. Note, the smoke from the wood chunks will likely burn out in about 1 hour, but the lamb ribs will have absorbed a good amount of the smoke into the core of the meat, so no need to add more.

6. Remove the lamb racks to a wire rack and let rest for at least 10 minutes. Carve into single chops and arrange on a serving platter. Drizzle the grilled scallion vinaigrette on top. Serve with barbecue sauce on the side.

Charred Scallion Vinaigrette
MAKES ABOUT 1 CUP

The rich, gamey flavor of the lamb ribs is subdued by the floral and charred flavor of this zesty scallion vinaigrette. It also goes great tossed with grilled corn cut off the cob.

Vegetable oil, for greasing the grill

2 bunches scallions

¼ cup extra-virgin olive oil, plus more for coating the scallions

1 teaspoon fine sea salt, plus more for seasoning

3 tablespoons apple cider vinegar

1. Preheat a charcoal or gas grill to medium-high heat (400 to 450°F). Take a few paper towels and fold them several times to make a thick square. Blot a small amount of vegetable oil on the paper towel, then carefully and quickly wipe the hot grates of the grill. This will create a nonstick grilling surface.

2. Drizzle the scallions with olive oil and season with salt. Lay the scallions on the hot grill and char on all sides, about 5 minutes. Remove the scallions to a cutting board and chop crosswise, leaving the stems on as they add a nice floral flavor. Transfer the scallions to a mixing bowl and add the vinegar, 1 teaspoon salt, and 3 tablespoons water. Stir to combine. Add the ¼ cup olive oil and mix well to combine. Serve on top of the lamb ribs.

Herb-Brined Smoked Turkey

SERVES 8 TO 10

During the holidays, I relish the simplicity of preparing a bone-in turkey breast instead of the whole dang bird! Smoking adds a rustic flair to the traditional (i.e., boring) roasted version and, frankly, does not take any more effort. Yet, it yields wow results. The advantage of a "turkey crown"—as the top part of the turkey breast is sometimes called—over a whole turkey is that it's quicker to cook and easier to carve. Plus, you don't have to worry about trying to cook the dark meat enough while not drying out the white meat. The breastbone acts as a natural roasting rack and helps to keep the lean white meat moist. Basic brine makes this turkey breast more flavorful and adds needed moisture and core flavor. Take note that the turkey is refrigerated in the brine for twenty-four hours, air-dried in the refrigerator for a day, and then smoked for several hours, so do plan your time accordingly. The brine is a simple combination of ingredients you probably have on hand. All you need is a large container and some refrigerator space. Serve with your favorite holiday sides.

1 cup kosher salt

½ cup packed light brown sugar

One 6-pound bone-in fresh turkey breast (turkey crown), rinsed and patted dry

4 cups low-sodium vegetable stock

One 2-inch piece fresh ginger, peeled and chopped

2 fresh flat-leaf parsley sprigs

2 fresh thyme sprigs

1 fresh rosemary sprig

1 fresh sage sprig

1 fresh savory sprig

1 small lemongrass stalk, tough outer layer removed and smashed

Peeled zest of 1 orange

1 tablespoon whole black peppercorns

1 teaspoon whole allspice

1 teaspoon dried red pepper flakes

Special Equipment

6 maplewood or cherrywood chunks

1. In a large stockpot, combine the salt and brown sugar with 16 cups warm water. Give it a stir to dissolve the brown sugar and salt. Put the turkey in the pot. Add the stock, 4 cups cold water, the ginger, parsley, thyme, rosemary, sage, savory, lemongrass, orange peel, peppercorns, allspice, and red pepper flakes. Put the pot in the refrigerator and brine the turkey for 24 hours—you may need to put a plate on top of the turkey to keep it submerged.

2. Remove the turkey from the brine, put it on a rimmed baking sheet, and pat dry with paper towels. Put the turkey in the refrigerator, uncovered, for 8 to 12 hours to air-dry; this will ultimately make the skin really crispy. Remove the turkey from the refrigerator 45 minutes before you plan to smoke.

3. Prepare and preheat the grill as a smoker to 275°F as instructed on page 194. Distribute the wood chunks around the coals and close the lid. Adjust the vents to maintain 275°F.

4. Place the turkey on the rack and close the lid. Smoke for about 3½ hours or until the internal temperature is about 160°F. Transfer the turkey to a wire rack, cover with aluminum foil, and rest until the internal temperature reaches 165°F, 20 to 30 minutes.

5. To carve, using a sharp knife, cut down either side of the breast bone, cut as close the bone as possible so you don't lose any meat. Keep cutting until the breast starts to come away from the bone and then use your hands to gently pull the breast away from the bone. Once the breast is pulled away from the breast bone, slice the breast fully away from the carcass. Repeat the process with the other breast. Put the breasts skin-side up on a cutting board and carve crosswise into slices.

Smoky Grilled Chicken Wings

SERVES 4 TO 6

Chicken wings have been a secret guilty pleasure of mine for ages. They are a favorite snack when I'm watching sports and want to really indulge and get a little messy. The downside is, most often chicken wings are breaded, fried, and far too greasy. My goal was to develop a version that had all of the crispy, crunchy goodness of a fried wing but with the rich flavor and tenderness you get from smoked wings. These wings have now become a favorite bar snack at Charcoal. You don't need an actual smoker to pull these beauties off and can transform your charcoal grill into a makeshift smoker simply by adding wood chips or chunks to the coals. Smoking on a charcoal grill is really easy to do, especially if you are already comfortable grilling with indirect heat. The wings smoke for a relatively short time, just enough to impart the smoky flavor, while crisping up on the grill at the same time. The chicken wings need to marinate for at least 12 hours, so plan accordingly. Serve with Smoked Paprika Chimichurri with Pickled Mustard Seeds (page 33) or Basque Vinegar (page 34) for dipping.

3 pounds (about 15) large chicken wings

1 cup Smoked Paprika Chimichurri with Pickled Mustard Seeds (page 33), plus more for serving

¼ cup Champagne vinegar

1 tablespoon dried red pepper flakes

Fine sea salt

Vegetable oil, for greasing the grill

Basque Vinegar (page 34) or Champagne vinegar, for serving

Special Equipment

4 applewood or cherrywood chunks or 2 large handfuls (about 1 cup) chips

1. Rinse the chicken wings and pat dry. With a sharp knife, remove the wing tip and discard; separate each wing at the joint into two pieces—the drumette and the flat piece. Put the wings in a container large enough to hold them (or in a large sealable plastic bag). In a small mixing bowl, combine the chimichurri, vinegar, and red pepper flakes. Pour the marinade over the wings and turn them over until evenly coated. Cover the wings (or seal the bag and press out the air) and marinate the wings in the refrigerator for at least 12 hours or up to 24. Take the chicken out of the refrigerator about 30 minutes before cooking so it can come up to room temperature.

2. Prepare and preheat the grill to 350°F, following the grill-smoking method on page 194. Distribute the wood chunks or chips around the coals and close the lid. Adjust the vents to maintain 350°F.

recipe continues

3. Remove the chicken wings from the marinade and season generously with salt. Take a few paper towels and fold them several times to make a thick square. Blot a small amount of vegetable oil on the paper towel, then carefully and quickly wipe the hot grates of the grill. This will create a nonstick grilling surface. Lay the wings directly on the grill in a single layer with about ¼ inch in between them. Close the lid of the grill.

4. Maintain a temperature of around 350°F, adjusting the vents accordingly. Flip the wings every 5 minutes to get an even golden brown and crispy skin. When you open the lid to turn the wings, flare-ups may occur. To control, close the vent slightly to limit the amount of oxygen or move the wings to another area of the grill. The entire process takes 15 to 20 minutes. Remove the wings from the grill and arrange on a serving platter. Serve with chimichurri and vinegar.

Smoked and Grilled Bone-In Short Ribs with Barbecue Sauce

SERVES 6 TO 8

Beef short ribs slow-smoked until rich and incredibly tender are the ultimate comfort food. Frankly, I'm no barbecue pitmaster, just a curious chef with a passion for creating new, tantalizing dishes. While I was never big into smoking, when I got the Big Green Egg I was intrigued by its versatility and started doing research and playing around with its capabilities. This was the first dish I ever smoked at home and I must have tested these ribs twenty times until they achieved melt-in-your mouth, fall-off-the-bone nirvana. The technique takes a bit of time—the ribs are first brined to add flavor and penetrate moisture, then air-dried to improve the meat's texture, smoked low and slow with sweet fruit wood, and finally brushed with barbecue sauce and seared on the grill to harden the crust and caramelize the fat (you may also stick the ribs under a broiler if you don't want to deal with setting up a grill after the smoking process). The resulting short ribs are a complex combination of smoky, crispy, fatty, and spicy with unparalleled tenderness. Trust me, most of the process requires unattended effort, and it's well worth the time! If by chance you have any leftover meat, chop it up and add to Grilled Vegetable Hash with Poached Egg and Yukon Potato (page 65).

1½ cups kosher salt

1¼ cups granulated sugar

Two 3-bone short rib plates (about 3½ pounds each), silver skin removed

4 fresh thyme sprigs

2 lemons, sliced

2 whole cayenne peppers, stemmed and halved lengthwise

1 garlic bulb, halved

1 bay leaf, preferably fresh

Vegetable oil, for greasing the grill

1 cup Red Wine Chipotle Barbecue Sauce (page 35)

Freshly ground black pepper

Special Equipment

6 applewood or cherrywood chunks

1. In a large stockpot, combine the salt and sugar with 4 cups warm water. Give it a stir to dissolve the sugar and salt. Put the short ribs in the pot. Add 12 cups cold water, the thyme, lemons, cayenne, garlic, and bay leaf. Put the pot in the refrigerator and brine the meat for 12 hours—you may need to put a plate on top of the ribs to keep them submerged.

2. Remove the ribs from the brine, put on a rimmed baking sheet fitted with a wire rack, and pat dry with paper towels. Put the ribs in the refrigerator, uncovered, for 8 to 12 hours to air-dry. Remove the ribs from the refrigerator 45 minutes before you plan on smoking.

3. Prepare and preheat the smoker to 250°F.

recipe continues

4. Place the short ribs on the rack, making sure there is ample space between each piece, and close the lid. Smoke the short ribs for about 6 hours or until the internal temperature is about 190°F. The temperature of the smoker needs to be maintained at around 250°F. You can control the temperature by working the vents to restrict the flow of oxygen. Make small adjustments—open the vent more to raise the temperature and close to reduce it. Remove the short ribs to a wire rack, cover loosely with aluminum foil, and let rest for at least 15 minutes.

5. In the meantime, preheat a charcoal or gas grill to medium heat (350°F).

6. Take a few paper towels and fold them several times to make a thick square. Blot a small amount of vegetable oil on the paper towel, then carefully and quickly wipe the hot grates of the grill. This will create a nonstick grilling surface. Lay the short ribs on the grill and brush generously with the barbecue sauce. Grill for 3 to 5 minutes, turning periodically, until the ribs are crispy and charred, taking care not to allow the sauce to burn. Remove the short ribs to a cutting board and let rest for 10 minutes. Carve the meat off the bones in one piece, leaving the three bones together. Cut the meat crosswise into slices. Arrange the bones on a serving platter and shingle the short rib slices over the top. Season with 4 or 5 turns of a peppermill. Serve any remaining barbecue sauce on the side.

Smoked Strawberries with Strawberry Water and Basil

SERVES 4

Dessert may not be the first thing you think of when you are cooking outdoors, but these sexy smoked berries lend a sweet-earthy finish to any summer meal. After a quick smoke in either a traditional smoker or charcoal grill rigged with hardwood chips or chunks, the fruit mellows out and is primed to release its natural juices when you gently cook it over simmering water. A consommé of sorts, the liquid that is released has intense strawberry flavor with an unexpected hint of smoky infusion.

3 pints fresh strawberries, stemmed and tops trimmed, quartered

Juice of 1 orange (about ¼ cup)

2 tablespoons sugar

2 tablespoons maple syrup

6 large fresh basil leaves

Vanilla ice cream, for serving

¼ cup store-bought granola

Special Equipment

3 applewood or maplewood chunks or 3 large handfuls (about 1½ cups) chips, plus a vegetable grill basket

1. Place 2 pints of the strawberries into a grill basket. Prepare and preheat the grill to 250°F, following the grill-smoking method on page 194. Distribute the wood chunks or chips around the coals and close the lid. Adjust the vents to maintain 250°F.

2. Put the grill basket of strawberries on the grate and close the lid. Smoke for 30 minutes. The strawberries will shrivel slightly and take on a smoked fragrance. Remove the berries from the smoker and set aside.

3. Create a double boiler to gently cook the smoked strawberries. Bring a saucepan of water to a simmer over medium-low heat. Put the smoked strawberries, ¼ cup cold water, the orange juice, sugar, maple syrup, and 3 basil leaves in a metal or glass heat-resistant bowl and set over the simmering water, without letting the bottom touch. Mix gently with a spoon, taking care not to smash the strawberries. Gently cook for 30 minutes to extract the natural juices from the strawberries.

4. Place the remaining pint of quartered strawberries in a medium mixing bowl. Strain the smoked strawberry liquid into the bowl and discard the pieces of smoked strawberries. Hand-tear the remaining 3 basil leaves and add to the strawberries; toss to combine. Refrigerate for at least for 15 minutes or until ready to serve.

5. To serve, spoon the macerated strawberries, including the liquid, into dessert bowls or martini glasses. Add a scoop of vanilla ice cream and sprinkle the granola on top.

Smoked Crème Brûlée

SERVES 8

As a French-trained chef, it's an interesting prospect to try to reinvent crème brûlée. I've likely made thousands of these bad boys in my long career, and so I enjoyed the challenge of creating a contemporary, smoked version that would stand out at Charcoal. Smoking the base of cream and milk over ice is my take on cold smoking and imparts an innovative dimension to the classic finish.

Special Equipment

4 applewood or maplewood chunks or chips or 6 large handfuls (about 3 cups) chips, kitchen torch, and eight 6-ounce ramekins or crème brûlée dishes

4 cups heavy cream

½ cup whole milk

10 large egg yolks, preferably organic and free-range

½ cup granulated sugar

1 whole vanilla bean

½ cup turbinado sugar

1. Prepare and preheat the grill to 200°F, following the grill-smoking method on page 194. Distribute the wood chips evenly around the coals and close the lid. Adjust the vents to maintain 200°F.

2. Combine the cream and milk in a medium metal bowl and set over another metal bowl filled with ice cubes. Place both bowls on top of the grill grate and close the lid. Smoke the cream and milk for 30 minutes. Remove from the grill and pour the cream mixture into a medium saucepan. Discard the bowl of water left from the ice.

3. Preheat the oven to 325°F.

4. In a large mixing bowl, cream together the egg yolks and granulated sugar with a whisk until the mixture is thick and pale yellow. Put the pot of smoked cream and milk over medium-low heat. Using a paring knife, split the vanilla bean down the middle, scrape out the seeds, and add them to saucepan. Bring the cream mixture to a brief simmer—do not boil or it can overflow. Remove from the heat and temper the yolks by gradually whisking the hot vanilla cream into the yolk-and-sugar mixture. Do not add the hot cream too quickly or the eggs will cook and begin to scramble. The custard should be thick enough to coat the back of a spoon. Strain the custard through a fine-mesh strainer into a clean bowl set over a bowl of ice. Stir to cool it down completely.

5. Divide the custard among eight 6-ounce ramekins or brûlée dishes, filling each about three-quarters full. Place the ramekins in a roasting pan and carefully fill the pan with enough water to come halfway up the sides of the ramekins. Bake until the custard is barely set around the edges and jiggles slightly when the dish is shaken, 50 to 55 minutes. You may want to cover the pan loosely with foil to prevent browning. Remove the pan from the oven and cool to room temperature. Transfer the ramekins to the refrigerator and chill for at least 2 hours, until completely cold.

6. Sprinkle 1 tablespoon of turbinado sugar on top of each chilled custard. Hold a kitchen torch 2 inches above the surface to brown the sugar and form a crust. Serve immediately.

Old-Fashioned with Smoked Ice

SERVES 1

I'm a fan of clean, classic cocktails, and the bourbon old-fashioned is one that is almost as easy to make as it is to drink. Gaining huge popularity since *Mad Men*'s Don Draper made this sipper into a bona fide food group, the intrinsic smokiness of whiskey begs for a devious partner in crime: enter smoked ice. It may seem like a counterintuitive step, but smoking ice cubes instead of the actual water produces ice with a pleasantly smoky flavor. Here's how it works: The original ice cubes end up melting during the smoking process and then have to be refrozen into new cubes once smoked. Smoke is attracted to cold objects more than warm ones and is therefore more likely to settle on ice rather than in liquid. To add wood-fired goodness to any spirit or cocktail, simply add the smoked cubes to drinks in the normal fashion, such as shaken in a martini or stirred in a Bloody Mary.

Special Equipment

8 mesquite wood chunks or 6 large handfuls (about 3 cups) chips

1 tray ice cubes

2 ounces bourbon, such as Maker's Mark

½ ounce Simple Syrup (see Note)

3 dashes orange bitters

2 dashes Angostura bitters

Peel of 1 orange

1. Prepare and preheat the grill to 225°F, following the grill-smoking method on page 194. Distribute the wood chunks/chips evenly around the coals and close the lid. Adjust the vents to maintain 225°F.

2. Put a tray of ice cubes in a shallow pan; high sides will block the flow of smoky air but the ice will melt, so make sure the sides are high enough to hold the water. Close the lid and smoke for about 1 hour. The ice will melt and produce an amber-colored water. Pour the smoked water back into the ice cube tray and freeze until solid.

3. To prepare the cocktail, combine the bourbon, simple syrup, and bitters in an old-fashioned/rocks glass. Stir with a bar spoon to combine. Add 3 or 4 of the smoked ice cubes and stir until cold and properly diluted, about 30 seconds. To flame the orange peel, hold a lit kitchen match between the peel and the cocktail, wave the orange skin over the flame, and gently squeeze so that the oil ignites and spritzes evenly over the surface of the cocktail. Insert the orange peel into the glass.

SIMPLE SYRUP

To make simple syrup, combine 1 cup warm water with 1 cup caster (superfine) sugar in a liquid measuring cup or glass jar. Stir well for a minute until the sugar is fully dissolved and the liquid is clear. Simple syrup keeps nearly indefinitely, covered, in the refrigerator.

OFF THE COALS

As much as my original game plan was to construct a restaurant that featured only the essence of charcoal, I believe a collection of salads, starters, and, of course, pasta rounds out the experience of cooking outdoors. As memorable as they are easy to make, all of the dishes in this chapter work well with fired foods, whether a fresh fish ceviche, hearty soup, or seasonal salad, and the dishes will ensure that guests clean their plates at your next backyard barbecue. Whether cooking outdoors or in the kitchen, keep these recipes in your rotating arsenal when feeding family or entertaining a group.

The multiuse vinaigrettes stand on their own right and are a blessing to have handy on the fridge door. Making your own vinaigrette is mandatory for a successful salad, and I please beg you not to overdress and drown salads in dressing; they should be a subtle, a quiet counterpoint to the greens.

◇◇

Little Gems with Flavors of Caesar

SERVE 4 TO 6

One of my first after-school jobs in high school was working the salad station at a local, artsy café in Venice Beach. Caesar salad was a mainstay on the menu and the place prided itself on mixing each one to order. I cranked out at least two hundred Caesar salads a day and learned the nuanced art of balance of components, teetering between the ratio of lettuce and garlicky-anchovy dressing. This rendition recipe rebuilds the classic, showcasing tender Little Gem lettuce, creamy buttermilk-anchovy dressing, and tender garlic chips.

Garlic Chips

2 elephant garlic cloves (see Note)

1 cup whole milk

2 cups vegetable oil

Salad

3 to 4 heads Little Gem lettuce

⅓ cup Buttermilk-Anchovy Dressing (recipe follows)

1 medium heirloom or beefsteak tomato, halved through the core and sliced ¼ inch thick lengthwise

2 hard-boiled egg yolks

3 tablespoons Lemon Bread Crumbs (page 77)

Freshly ground black pepper

1. Make the garlic chips: Use a small truffle/chocolate shaver or a mandoline to very carefully slice the garlic lengthwise into thin slivers. Put the garlic in a small saucepan with the milk and bring to a boil to soften it and remove a bit of the bitterness. After the milk comes to a boil, strain it out, rinse the garlic in cold water, and dry well on paper towels.

2. Put the garlic in a small sauté pan or pot and pour in the vegetable oil to cover. Place over medium-high heat. Bring the oil and garlic gently up to a sizzle, swirling the pan around and stirring to prevent the garlic from getting too brown, too fast. Pay close attention! Cook until the garlic is just crisp and light golden brown, under 2 minutes. Line a plate with paper towels. Set a mesh strainer over a heatproof bowl and pour the garlic chips and oil through it. Lay the garlic chips on the paper towels to drain. The chips will become crispier as they cool. The garlic oil may be reserved for other sautés and dressings.

3. Make the salad: Fill a large bowl with ice water. Trim off the bottom of each lettuce head so that you can easily separate the leaves and add

Ingredient Note: Elephant Garlic

As the name suggests, elephant garlic is twice the size as regular garlic, with only about five cloves per bulb. The giant size of elephant garlic cloves means you can slice them more easily and more safely into nice slivers for making the salad chips. Elephant garlic is actually not a true garlic variety and is related to leeks. It has a mild garlic flavor.

recipe continues

them to the ice water. Swish the leaves around and allow to sit in the water for 10 minutes to "shock" them. Drain the lettuce and put it in a salad spinner lined with paper towels—you may have to do this in batches so as not to overcrowd the spinner. Spin the lettuce in the salad spinner to remove excess water. Lay the lettuce out on a baking sheet lined with paper towels to remove any remaining moisture—dry lettuce is key for the dressing to coat properly.

4. Hand-tear the lettuce if necessary, and put it into a large mixing bowl. Add half of the dressing and toss to coat evenly. Add the tomatoes and the remaining dressing; toss again to fully incorporate. Transfer the salad to a large serving platter. Using a Microplane, evenly grate the egg yolks on top of the salad; sprinkle with the bread crumbs and garlic chips. Season with 6 turns of a peppermill. Serve immediately.

Buttermilk-Anchovy Dressing

MAKES 1½ CUPS

A bagna cauda of sorts, the anchovy oil is the key backbone of this dressing, which makes a great bread spread or crudité dip on its own. Cured white anchovy is far superior to the tinned variety and has a milder, less fishy taste. You can find it in Spanish, Italian, or gourmet markets, as well as online.

Anchovy Oil

One 7-ounce container marinated white anchovy fillets (boquerones), drained and chopped

¼ cup finely chopped fresh chives

½ cup extra-virgin olive oil

1 small shallot, minced

1 garlic clove, minced after removing the germ (see Note, page 31)

Buttermilk Dressing

½ cup mayonnaise

½ cup buttermilk

2 teaspoons Dijon mustard

Finely grated zest of 1 lemon

Juice of ½ lemon

Fine sea salt

⅓ cup Anchovy Oil

Freshly ground black pepper

1. Make the anchovy oil: Combine the chopped anchovies and chives in a jar with a tight-fitting lid. In a small saucepan, combine the olive oil, shallot, and garlic and place over medium-low heat. Heat slowly, swirling the pan around, until small bubbles start to pop up around the shallot and garlic and they become translucent, about 3 minutes. Pour the oil mixture into the jar over the anchovies and chives. Stir to combine thoroughly. Cool to room temperature before covering and storing in the refrigerator. Shake the oil periodically. The anchovy oil keeps for up to 2 weeks covered in the refrigerator. Reserve ⅓ cup for the buttermilk dressing. The remaining can be used as a flavorful bread or vegetable dip.

2. Make the buttermilk dressing: In a mixing bowl, combine the mayonnaise, buttermilk, mustard, lemon zest, lemon juice, and anchovy oil. Mix with a small whisk or spoon until smooth and creamy. Season with 6 turns of a peppermill. Cover and refrigerate for at least 1 hour before serving. The dressing keeps for up to 1 week, covered, in the refrigerator.

Collard Greens with Yam, Shaved Onion, Aged Cheddar, and Raisin-Caper Vinaigrette

SERVES 4 TO 6

I think people are intimidated by collard greens because they think they need to cook them for an extremely long time. Collard greens actually have a very similar flavor profile to kale, which has become the prevalent, sturdy green featured in salads across the country. Massaging the collards is key to minimizing any bitterness and tenderizing the leaves, so you don't need to chew for minutes to break them down. The flavor of raw collard greens combines perfectly with tender roasted yams and sharp aged Cheddar in this hearty starter or main-meal salad. Dress with the Raisin-Caper Vinaigrette about 5 minutes before you plan to serve, so it has a chance to soak into the leaves and soften them a bit. Collard's peppery kick absorbs this sweet-tart vinaigrette to create a supple salad with vibrant flavor.

1 large red garnet yam or sweet potato, peeled and cut into ¾-inch cubes

1½ teaspoons light brown sugar

1 teaspoon fine sea salt

1 tablespoon extra-virgin olive oil

2 bunches collard greens, stemmed

½ sweet onion, thinly sliced on a mandoline

10 assorted radishes, stemmed and thinly sliced on a mandoline

¾ cup Raisin-Caper Vinaigrette (recipe follows)

1½ cups shredded aged Cheddar cheese

½ cup Lemon Bread Crumbs (page 77)

1. Preheat the oven to 475°F. Line a rimmed baking sheet with parchment paper.

2. Put the yam cubes in a medium mixing bowl and toss with the brown sugar and salt. Drizzle with the olive oil and toss again to coat. Spread the yams out on the prepared baking sheet. Bake until the yams are fork-tender and slightly caramelized, about 20 minutes. Set aside to cool.

3. Cut the leaves off the center ribs of the collard greens. Discard the ribs and stack up piles of the leaves on top of one another. Cut the collards down the center lengthwise and then crosswise into ½-inch pieces. Fill a large bowl with ice water. Add the collards to the water and swish around to allow the sand to fall to the bottom of the bowl. Pull out the collards with your hands, taking care not to disturb the sediment at the bottom of the bowl, and lay out on a baking sheet lined with paper towels to dry. Using your hands, massage the greens for about 2 minutes to soften and tenderize the leaves.

4. Steep the sliced onions and radishes in ice water for about 10 minutes to crisp them up. Drain and then pat dry with paper towels.

5. Put the dried collard greens into a serving bowl. Add the onion, radishes, and cooled yams. Drizzle with the vinaigrette and toss to coat evenly. Add the Cheddar and toss again to combine. Divide the salad among plates or bowls and garnish with the bread crumbs.

recipe continues

Raisin-Caper Vinaigrette

MAKES ABOUT 2 CUPS

This sweet-tangy vinaigrette keeps up to 1 month, covered, in the refrigerator and marries well with other bitter peppery greens, like dandelion or kale. It's thick enough to also sub as a cold sauce drizzled over grilled shrimp, scallops, or chicken.

¼ cup golden raisins

¼ cup non-pareil capers, drained

1 tablespoon Dijon mustard

1 garlic clove, minced after removing the germ (see Note, page 31)

½ cup freshly squeezed lemon juice

½ cup grapeseed oil

¼ cup extra-virgin olive oil

Combine the raisins, capers, mustard, garlic, lemon juice, and ¼ cup water in a blender and blend on medium speed until completely smooth. Reduce to low speed and, with the motor running, drizzle in the grapeseed oil and olive oil in a slow, steady stream until emulsified. The vinaigrette may be stored, covered, in the refrigerator for up to 1 month. Shake to re-emulsify before using.

Arugula and Radicchio with Sliced Apple, Feta Cheese, and Roasted Pumpkin Vinaigrette

SERVES 4 TO 6

Crisp apple, salty feta, and peppery greens make for a colorful and refreshing main or side salad bursting with contrasting flavor and texture. This is a fall favorite of mine, but feel free to rotate seasonal fruit throughout the year by switching out the apples for fresh peaches or strawberries in summer, or blood orange segments in winter.

3½ cups wild arugula (about 12 ounces)

1 head radicchio, cut into quarters through the core and then crosswise into 1-inch pieces

½ cup watercress leaves

1 Pink Lady apple, halved and thinly sliced crosswise on a mandoline

½ cup Roasted Pumpkin Vinaigrette (recipe follows)

½ cup crumbled feta cheese, preferably French

2 tablespoons pumpkin seeds (pepitas), toasted

Pinch of fine sea salt and freshly ground black pepper

In a large serving bowl, combine the arugula, radicchio, watercress, and apple. Toss well with the vinaigrette to coat evenly. Sprinkle in the feta and pumpkin seeds, and toss again to distribute evenly. Season lightly with salt and 6 turns of a peppermill. Serve immediately.

Roasted Pumpkin Vinaigrette

MAKES ABOUT 2 CUPS

Thick, vibrantly hued, and wonderfully versatile, this pumpkin vinaigrette is no slouch—it stands up tall to sturdy greens and also complements cold-weather produce, such as roasted winter squash or root vegetables, like carrots or turnips. Due to the vinaigrette's viscosity, try it as delicious spread on post-Thanksgiving turkey sandwiches. If fresh pumpkin is not in season, substitute ½ cup canned pure pumpkin puree in the vinaigrette.

½ small sugar pumpkin (about 1 pound)

Extra-virgin olive oil

¼ teaspoon fine sea salt, plus more for baking the pumpkin

Freshly ground black pepper

1 tablespoon Dijon mustard

1 garlic clove, crushed into a paste after removing the germ (see Note, page 31)

½ shallot, finely diced

Freshly ground black pepper

¼ cup apple cider vinegar

¼ cup balsamic vinegar

Juice of ½ lemon

¾ cup grapeseed oil

½ cup pumpkin seed oil

1. Preheat the oven to 350°F.

2. Using a sharp knife, cut off the crown of the pumpkin and discard it. Cut the pumpkin into 1-inch wedges and remove the seeds. Lay the pumpkin slices on a rimmed baking sheet, drizzle with olive oil, and season with salt and pepper. Turn the pumpkin over and repeat on the other side. Bake until the pumpkin is completely cooked and soft enough to be pureed, about 30 minutes. Let cool.

3. Remove the skin from the pumpkin and discard. Transfer the pumpkin flesh to a blender, preferably a Vitamix, and puree until completely smooth.

4. Measure ½ cup of pumpkin puree for the vinaigrette. (Reserve remaining puree for another use.) In a large jar or container with a tight-fitting lid, combine ½ cup of the pumpkin puree, the mustard, garlic, shallot, ¼ teaspoon salt, and 6 turns of a peppermill—adding salt to the base of the vinaigrette before the oil is key so it dissolves. Pour in the vinegars, lemon juice, and ¼ cup water. Add the grapeseed oil and pumpkin seed oil, secure the lid, and shake well again until fully emulsified. Shake well before dressing the salad. The vinaigrette keeps, covered, in the refrigerator for 1 week.

Snapper Ceviche with Citrus and Coconut

SERVES 4 TO 6

In a nutshell, ceviche is seafood that is prepared by marinating it in citrus juice, which makes the fish more opaque and firm, just as if it had been cooked with heat. I like to keep my recipe pretty straightforward, with fresh, mild snapper being a favorite fish. If you want to play around with seafood, striped bass, scallops, and halibut are all the right texture. Whichever you choose, it's important to start with the freshest, cleanest fish possible. There is no need to marinate for hours or cook the seafood beforehand. The bright, refreshing combo of lime, lemon, and orange, with creamy avocado and sweet mango, exemplifies the balance of texture, flavor, and visual appeal. If I had to describe it, I'd say it tastes like sashimi salsa. The process of changing the citrus juice a couple of times evenly "cooks" the fish and gets rid of the milky residue that tends to leach out of the fish, for a cleaner, brighter tropical flavor. Mint is a fantastic alternative to cilantro, which can be unappetizing to some palates.

1 pound fresh, skinless snapper fillets, such as Tai or red

Fine sea salt

1 cup freshly squeezed lime juice (about 4 limes)

½ cup freshly squeezed lemon juice (about 3 lemons)

½ cup freshly squeezed orange juice (about 1 orange)

½ ripe and firm mango, halved, pitted, peeled, and diced small

½ ripe and firm avocado, halved, pitted, peeled, and diced small

2 small plum (Roma) tomatoes, seeded and diced small

2 tablespoons minced red onion

½ jalapeño, seeded and minced

½ cup coconut water

2 tablespoons finely chopped fresh mint leaves

Fleur de sel

¼ teaspoon Piment d'Espelette (see Note, page 34) or cayenne

Endive spears, butter lettuce leaves, plantain chips, or sweet potato chips, for serving

1. Set a wire rack on a baking sheet and lay the snapper fillets on top. Season both sides of the fish with salt and set aside, uncovered, for 45 minutes; the salt will pull out some of the natural moisture of the fish and concentrate the sweet snapper flavor.

2. Rinse the fish with cold water and pat dry with paper towels. Cut the fillets into ¼-inch dice and put into a nonreactive glass or stainless steel bowl. Pour in ½ cup of the lime juice, ¼ cup lemon juice, and ¼ cup of the orange juice. Cover and refrigerate for 10 minutes. Pour out the juice and repeat soaking the fish with the remaining ½ cup lime juice, ¼ cup lemon juice, and ¼ cup orange juice for 10 minutes, one more time. Drain out the second batch of citrus juice. Add the mango, avocado, tomatoes, onion, jalapeño, and coconut water to the marinated fish. Toss to combine and refrigerate for 15 minutes for the flavors to marry. Mix in the mint and season with a pinch of fleur de sel and the Piment d'Espelette.

3. Using a slotted spoon, spoon the ceviche into a serving bowl or small individual bowls. Serve immediately with lettuce or chips.

Beef Tartare with Seeds and Spices

SERVES 4 TO 6

One of the delights I never miss out on when traveling to France is the great classic *Tartare de Boeuf* mixed tableside—it's just so damn delicious! When I opened Charcoal, I wanted to showcase a unique tartare menu selection, grounded by the original French specialty prepared with raw beef. The truth about beef tartare is that it's totally safe to make at home, but since you're not cooking the stuff, the quality of the beef you buy matters more than ever. If you've got a local butcher or specialty meat shop, this is the time to pay a visit. My standard roster of flavors includes fresh herbs, salty cornichons and capers, mustard, and finely chopped shallot; the addition of crunchy pumpkin and sunflower seeds and spicy chili oil gives the meat mixture a modern, fresh take. You'll need a meat grinder to execute the fluffy, snowy texture that is key for this light tartare.

8 ounces high-quality beef, such as New York strip or tenderloin, sinew removed, cut into chunks

2 ounces beef fat, coarsely chopped

8 cornichons, coarsely chopped

2 tablespoons non-pareil capers, drained

1 small shallot, minced

2 tablespoons finely chopped fresh chives

2 tablespoons finely chopped fresh flat-leaf parsley

Finely grated zest of 1 lemon

1 tablespoon Dijon mustard

1 teaspoon fine sea salt

1 teaspoon Piment d'Espelette (see Note, page 34) or cayenne

2 teaspoons Asian chili oil

2 tablespoons store-bought puffed quinoa

1 tablespoon toasted pumpkin seeds (pepitas)

1 tablespoon toasted sunflower or hemp seeds

½ cup Lemon Aioli (page 152)

Charcoal Flatbread (page 185), grilled or toasted sliced baguette, for serving

1. In a large mixing bowl, combine the steak, beef fat, cornichons, capers, shallot, chives, parsley, lemon zest, mustard, salt, and Piment d'Espelette. Toss all of the ingredients until thoroughly combined. Freeze until the mixture is cold to the touch but not frozen, about 30 minutes.

2. Set a serving bowl underneath a meat grinder fitted with a coarse plate—it's best if the meat mixture is ground directly into what you plan on serving in for the finest texture and display.

3. Working in batches, grind the beef mixture into the serving bowl, moving the bowl around to catch the free-falling tartare emerging from the grinder. You want to be sure the tartare is evenly distributed in the serving bowl. Drizzle the tartare with the chili oil and top with puffed quinoa, pumpkin seeds, and sunflower seeds. Spread the aioli on the toasted bread and arrange on a separate platter for guests to top with the beef tartare. Serve immediately, family-style.

Black Kale and White Bean Soup

SERVES 4 TO 6

Long before kale became cool, I created this vegetarian soup when my son was working on a school project about meatless Mondays. Packed with vegetables and creamy white beans, this hearty soup satisfies even the biggest carnivores. Also known as Tuscan, dinosaur, lacinato, and cavolo nero, black kale is an Italian variety with long, spiky, ruffled, deep green leaves. It is less bitter than curly kale with an earthier, more delicate taste. This soup tastes even better on the second day and will keep for 4 or 5 days in the refrigerator (and also freezes well). Top with a gooey poached egg for added decadence. If you are missing the meat, cut up a couple of Eisenhower Sausages (see Eisenhower Sausage and Peppers Hero, page 167) and mix into the soup before serving.

½ pound dried white beans, such as cannellini or Great Northern

¼ sweet onion, with skin, plus 1 small sweet onion, finely diced

½ carrot, not cut up, plus 1 carrot, halved lengthwise and chopped ¼ inch thick

1 garlic clove, with skin, plus 2 garlic cloves, minced after removing the germ (see Note, page 31)

Fine sea salt

2 tablespoons grapeseed oil

1 celery stalk, ends trimmed and halved lengthwise and sliced ¼ inch thick

6 shiitake mushrooms, wiped of grit, stemmed, halved, and cut crosswise

One 14½-ounce can diced tomatoes, with juice

8 cups low-sodium vegetable or chicken stock

Bouquet garni (6 parsley sprigs, 4 thyme sprigs, 2 sage sprigs, and 1 rosemary sprig tied together with kitchen string)

½ pound black kale (about 2 bunches), center ribs removed, leaves sliced crosswise

Crusty bread, for serving

Lemon wedges, chopped parsley, chopped scallions, and grated Parmesan, for serving

1. Cover the beans with 2 inches of cool water in a medium saucepan and bring to a boil over medium-high heat. Once the water comes to a boil, cover, and remove from the heat, and let stand for 30 minutes. Drain the beans in a colander and rinse with cool water. Put the beans back into the pot and add the quarter onion, half carrot, and garlic clove with skin. Cover the beans and aromatics with cold water and bring to a boil over medium-high heat. Reduce to medium-low heat and bring down to just below a simmer. Cook, uncovered, for 30 minutes, skimming the impurities that rise to the surface. Season the beans with 2 teaspoons of salt. Continue to gently simmer until the beans are tender but not broken apart, about 15 minutes. Drain and set aside.

2. Coat the bottom of a soup pot with the grapeseed oil and place over medium-low heat. Add the sweet onion and minced garlic; cook and stir until translucent, 3 to 4 minutes. Add the chopped carrot and sauté for 1 minute. Add the celery and mushrooms, season with a pinch of salt, and continue to cook, stirring often, until the

recipe continues

vegetables are tender, about 5 minutes. Stir in the tomatoes and juice from the can; add another pinch of salt and cook, stirring often, until the tomatoes have cooked down slightly, about 5 minutes.

boil. Reduce the heat to medium and simmer, uncovered, for 20 minutes, stirring periodically. Stir in the kale and reserved beans. Simmer until the kale is wilted and beans heated through, 5 to 10 minutes.

3. Pour in the stock and toss the boquet garni into a pot; season lightly with salt. Raise the heat to medium-high and bring the soup to a

4. Discard the bouquet garni. Ladle the soup into bowls and serve with crusty bread and toppings for guests to add as they like.

Linguine with Avocado Pesto and Tomato

SERVES 4

My California twist on a traditional Italian favorite, I put this emerald green pesto-pasta on the menu as a seasonal spring special and it immediately became a bestselling staple. Creamy avocado is blended with vibrant fresh basil, arugula, and spinach. This out-of-the-ordinary rendition of an uncooked pasta sauce boasts a bright, herbaceous flavor and silky texture from the healthy fat found in avocados. If you want to get fancy, top with a dollop of decadent Dungeness crab, caviar, or shaved truffles. You can also skip the pasta and easily spread the avocado pesto on toasted baguette slices for the quintessential California avocado toast.

1 cup baby arugula leaves

1 cup baby spinach leaves

1 cup packed fresh basil leaves, plus 4 leaves for serving

2 ripe and firm avocados, halved, pitted, peeled, and cut into chunks

¼ cup toasted unsalted pistachios

¼ cup toasted unsalted cashews

2 garlic cloves, crushed after removing the germ (see Note, page 31)

Juice of 1 lemon

Fine sea salt and freshly ground black pepper

¼ cup extra-virgin olive oil

1 cup grated Parmesan cheese

1 pound dry linguine

12 grape tomatoes, halved lengthwise

3 tablespoons Lemon Bread Crumbs (page 77), for garnish

1. In the bowl of a food processor, combine the arugula, spinach, basil, avocados, pistachios, cashews, garlic, and lemon juice; season lightly with salt and 2 turns of a peppermill. Pulse until a paste forms, pushing the greens down the sides of the bowl as needed. With the motor running, pour in the olive oil and puree until well blended, smooth, and bright green.

Add the Parmesan and pulse a few times to incorporate. If you're not going to use the pesto immediately, press a piece of plastic wrap against the surface before refrigerating to keep it from oxidizing. The pesto will keep, covered, in the refrigerator for up to 2 days.

2. Bring a large pot of well-salted water to a boil over high heat and add the pasta. Give the pasta a good stir and cook for 12 minutes or until tender yet firm (al dente). Reserve 1 cup of the starchy pasta water and drain the linguine in a colander. Put the linguine in a serving bowl, add the pesto, and toss well until the strands are evenly coated. Add the tomatoes and toss again to distribute evenly. If the pasta looks too thick, add the reserved pasta water, a little at a time, and toss to loosen it up and create a silky pesto. Sprinkle the bread crumbs on top. Stack the remaining 4 basil leaves on top of one another and roll up lengthwise, like a cigar. Cut crosswise into fine ribbons (chiffonade) and scatter over the pasta before serving.

Blueberry and Yuzu Trifle

SERVES 6

With layers of sweetened blueberries, soft sponge cake, and fluffy whipped cream, this do-ahead dessert is the perfect finish to a summer super. A fun twist of the classic pairing of blueberry and lemon, tart yuzu juice injects a distinctive citrus flavor and aroma that adds an exotic element to this trifle. You can prepare all of the components ahead of time and assemble shortly before serving. I like to serve guests individual trifles built in clear 12-ounce rocks glasses for an impressive presentation.

Biscuit-Sponge Cake

¼ cup sugar

3 large egg whites, preferably organic and free-range, at room temperature

3 large egg yolks, preferably organic and free-range

¼ cup all-purpose flour

Nonstick cooking spray

Blueberry Yuzu Compote

½ cup plus 1 tablespoon sugar

3½ teaspoons apple pectin powder

4 pints blueberries, rinsed and dried

½ cup yuzu juice, plus more for brushing

Pastry Cream

4 large egg yolks, preferably organic and free-range

2 large eggs, preferably organic and free-range

5 teaspoons cornstarch

4 tablespoons sugar

2 cups milk

1 cup heavy cream

1 tablespoon pure vanilla extract

Whipped Cream

1 cup heavy cream, cold

1 teaspoon pure vanilla extract

2 tablespoons confectioners' sugar

1. Make the biscuit-sponge cake: Combine the sugar and egg whites in the bowl of a standing mixer fitted with a wire whisk attachment. Whip on medium-high speed until stiff peaks form. Slow to lowest speed and add the egg yolks, one by one, until they are completely incorporated. Remove the bowl from the mixer and fold in the flour with a rubber spatula, 1 tablespoon at a time, until fully incorporated.

2. Preheat the oven to 300°F. Coat a 9 x 13-inch baking dish with nonstick spray, and then lay a piece of parchment paper on top to cover—the spray will keep the parchment stuck in place in the pan.

3. Spread the batter in an even layer to reach the sides of the pan. Bake for 15 to 20 minutes or until the cake is light golden brown and bounces back to the touch. Cool completely in the pan. May be made 1 day ahead, covered, at room temperature.

4. Make the blueberry yuzu compote: Mix the sugar and pectin in a small bowl with your fingers to thoroughly combine. Put 3 pints of the blueberries in a saucepan and place over medium heat. Cook and stir until the berries

recipe continues

start to soften, 5 to 8 minutes. Sprinkle in the pectin mixture and continue to cook and stir until the blueberries release their juices and look jam-like, about 3 minutes. Pour in the yuzu juice and continue to simmer and stir until thick, 12 to 15 minutes. Remove from the heat and fold in the remaining pint of blueberries. Set aside at room temperature to cool completely. May be made up to 1 day ahead and stored covered in the refrigerator.

5. Make the pastry cream: In a large bowl, cream together the egg yolks, eggs, cornstarch, and 2 tablespoons of the sugar with a whisk until the mixture is thick and pale yellow, about 2 minutes.

6. Combine the milk, cream, remaining 2 tablespoons sugar, and vanilla in a medium saucepan over medium-low heat. Bring to a brief simmer but do not boil, or it might overflow. Using a large ladle or measuring cup, temper the eggs by gradually whisking half of the hot vanilla cream into the egg-and-sugar mixture. Do not add the hot cream too quickly or the eggs will cook and begin to scramble. Add the tempered eggs back into the pot and whisk over medium-low heat until the mixture begins to thicken and the raw taste of the cornstarch is cooked out, about 5 minutes. Remove from the heat. Strain the custard through a fine-mesh strainer into a clean bowl set over a bowl of ice. Stir to cool it down completely. Cover and store in the refrigerator until ready to use. Note that you will likely have more pastry cream than you need for the trifles. Any leftover can be spread on toast with fruit jam or dolloped on fresh fruit.

7. Make the whipped cream: Chill a mixing bowl and wire whisk in the freezer for 10 minutes before beginning. Whisk the cream and vanilla in the chilled bowl until it begins to foam and thicken up. Add the confectioners' sugar and continue to beat until stiff peaks form. Do not over-whip. Cover and store in the refrigerator until ready to use.

8. To build the trifles: Using a rocks glass that you will be serving in, invert the rim of the glass on top of the cake and punch out 6 circles. Brush the tops of the cake circles with yuzu juice to moisten. Fold a dish towel on the counter where you are layering the trifles. Working with 1 rocks glass at a time, spoon ¼ cup of the pastry cream into the bottom of the glass. Tap the glass on the folded towel to flatten the pastry cream into an even layer. Next, top the pastry cream with 3 tablespoons of the blueberry compote and gently spread out evenly with the back of a teaspoon. Put a disk of cake on top, pressing down gently with your fingers so there is not a gap between the compote and cake. Repeat the process with the pastry cream and compote to create a second layer. To finish, top each trifle with ¼ cup of the whipped cream (you may use a pastry bag fitted with a large round tip or a teaspoon to dollop on top). Use a knife or flat spatula to level off the cream with the rim of the glass. Repeat with the remaining servings. The trifles can easily be made 1 day before you plan to serve.

The Bandit

SERVES 1

Bourbon is my favorite whiskey, not only for sipping straight or on the rocks, but the oaky flavor is perfect for mixing into cocktails too. I can't deal with drinks that try too hard, are in-your-face abrasive, and sugary sweet. This straightforward cocktail is smooth, well balanced, and understated, and doesn't require special bar equipment. Pomegranate syrup, a.k.a. grenadine, is a key ingredient for a wide range of cocktails, from the classic Jack Rose to tiki-inspired rum drinks. House-made grenadine, unlike the store-bought stuff, gives drinks a rosy hue and vibrant, fruity flavor.

Pomegranate Syrup

½ cup pomegranate juice

½ cup caster (superfine) sugar

1½ ounces bourbon, such as Buffalo Trace

¾ ounce dry vermouth, such as Dolin

¾ ounce freshly squeezed lemon juice

¾ ounce pomegranate syrup

1 large ice cube or sphere

1. To prepare the pomegranate syrup: Combine the pomegranate juice and sugar in a liquid measuring cup. Stir to dissolve the sugar.

2. Combine the bourbon, vermouth, lemon juice, and pomegranate syrup in a mixing glass filled with ice. Stir with a bar spoon until cold and properly diluted, about 30 seconds. Put the large ice cube into an old-fashioned/rocks glass. Strain the cocktail over top and serve.

Les Restes

SERVES 1

The French version of leftovers, "The Rest" is a cocktail that evolved from a happy accident. Local mixologist Pablo Moix consulted on revamping our bar program at Charcoal, and when all was said and done, we found we had a surplus of vodka and lychee juice left over from the previous menu. So instead of wasting product, Pablo dreamed up this refreshing, floral cocktail to utilize the remains of the day. As luck would have it, it's become one of our most popular drinks.

2 ounces vodka

¾ ounce lychee juice

½ ounce Simple Syrup (page 221)

1 large egg white

3 dashes Angostura bitters

1 seedless grape, cut crosswise

Combine the vodka, lychee juice, simple syrup, and egg white in a shaker and fill with ice. Shake vigorously until the egg white has velvety foam. Strain the cocktail into a coup or martini glass. Drop the bitters on top in a triangle, which will settle in the foam of the cocktail. Using a straw or toothpick, swirl the bitters into a simple design in the frothy white top. Float the grape slices on top for garnish.

Nightcap

SERVES 1

Cynar is an Italian amaro named after one of its key ingredients—artichoke. Cynar doesn't really taste like artichokes but does boast a botanical/vegetal quality. Super simple to make as an after-dinner drink, the chocolaty and cherry notes in the espresso really complement the pleasing bitterness characteristic of Cynar.

3 ounces (double shot) brewed espresso

¼ cup cold water

1½ ounces Cynar

1 large ice cube or sphere

Peel of 1 orange

1. Combine the espresso and water in a liquid measuring cup. Cool to room temperature.

2. To prepare the cocktail: Combine 1 ounce of the espresso mixture and the Cynar in an old-fashioned/rocks glass. Stir with a bar spoon to combine. Add the large ice cube and stir until cold and properly diluted, about 30 seconds. Twist an orange peel over the surface of the cocktail and drop it into the glass.

CONVERSION CHART

All conversions have been rounded up or down to the nearest whole number.

LIQUID MEASURES

US	Milliliters
1 teaspoon	5
2 teaspoons	10
1 tablespoon	14
2 tablespoons	28
¼ cup	56
½ cup	120
⅓ cup	170
1 cup	240
1¼ cups	280
1½ cups	340
2 cups	450
2¼ cups	500, ½ liter
2½ cups	560
3 cups	675
3½ cups	750
3¾ cups	840
4 cups or 1 quart	900
4¼ cups	1000, 1 liter
5 cups	1120

WEIGHT MEASURES

Ounces	Pounds	Grams	Kilos
1		28	
2		56	
3½		100	
4	¼	112	
5		140	
6		168	
8	½	225	
9		250	¼
12	¾	340	
16	1	450	
18		500	½
20	1¼	560	
24	1½	675	
27		750	¾
28	1¾	780	
32	2	900	
36	2¼	1000	
40	2½	1100	1
48	3	1350	
54		1500	1½

OVEN TEMPERATURE EQUIVALENTS

Farenheit	Celcius	Gas Mark	Description
225	110	¼	Cool
250	130	½	
275	140	1	Very slow
300	150	2	
325	170	3	Slow
350	180	4	Moderate
375	190	5	
400	200	6	Moderately hot
425	220	7	Fairly hot
450	230	8	Hot
475	240	9	Very hot
500	250	10	Extremely hot

ACKNOWLEDGMENTS

Josiah

Thank you to my team for your enthusiasm and untiring effort in making this book happen.

To Joe Johnson, for his time spent developing the recipes and bringing flavors to the table that have made Charcoal Venice what it is. Most important, for his relentless and unwavering dedication and passion that gets put into Charcoal.

Danny Freeman, for his tireless energy in prepping and cooking for the shoot and for being a force to be reckoned with in the kitchen.

To Rebecca Barone, who organized and managed this project each step of the way and for helping recipe test the book.

Maya Maniktala, for her support and help with this book from beginning to end.

Ken Takayama, for his continued culinary support and expertise.

Stan Lee, who captured the essence of Charcoal in each of the photos in this book.

Michael Cimarusti, for allowing us to shoot at Cape Seafood & Provisions and for furthering the education of ocean sustainability.

To JoAnn Cianciulli, who spent many, many hours taking my techniques and putting them into words, and for taking my words and turning them into beautifully written stories.

Nicole Tourtelot and Lucia Watson, for understanding my vision and for making this venture as seamless as possible.

Heath Ceramics and Staub, for heightening the beauty of our dishes with each of their plates, bowls, and pots used in this book.

JoAnn

Loving what I do everyday is the absolute greatest joy in my life. Writing cookbooks and producing food television shows is a hybrid career that characterizes my passion for cooking in a unique way. As a result, I'm fortunate to collaborate closely with the top talent in the culinary world. This book would not have been possible without the intelligence and loyalty of superstar chef Josiah Citrin. Josiah, thank you for letting me climb inside your brilliant brain and put your full and delicious thoughts on paper. You are a great professional mentor and it's been a true joy to work with you on countless levels.

I am incredibly proud of this project. A culmination of patience, time, and hard work and a number of people gave me vital support along the way. I must give a shout-out to the talented people who contributed to this book in one way or another:

Lucia Watson, our skillful editor, and her remarkable team at Penguin/Avery, for producing such a beautiful book.

Laura Nolan, my top-notch literary agent, for always telling it like it is and for having the keen ability to recognize the right fit between chef and writer.

My mother, Gloria, for fighting the good fight.

My auntie Grace, for her unwavering love, encouragement, and her gracious, indefatigable spirit.

INDEX

Page numbers in *italics* refer to photos.

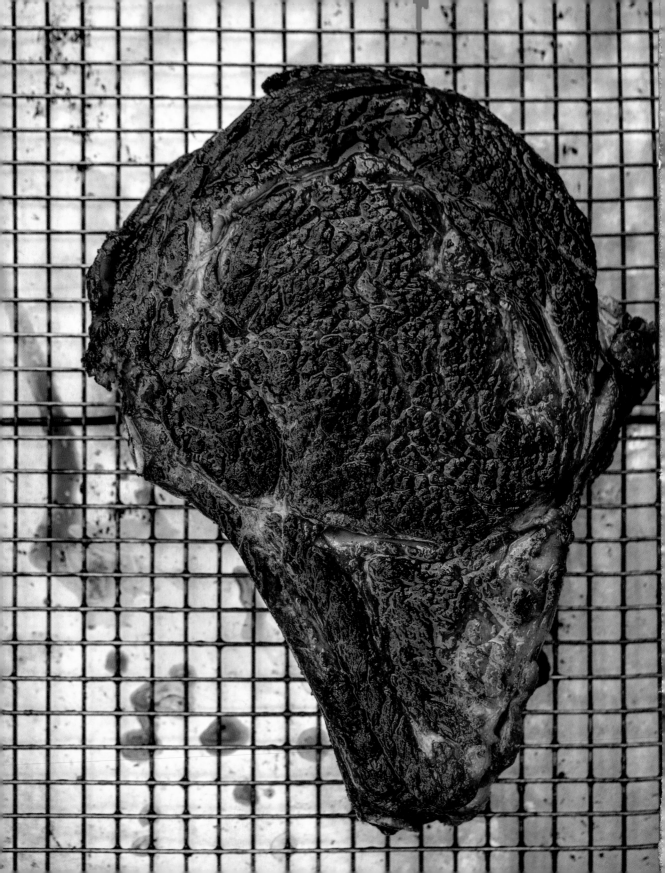